She will be called "woman,"
because she was taken from "man."

Genesis 2:23 NLT

Beautiful daughter, though female
was created last, she is not the least.
You began in God's image
and were reborn His daughter.
Yet I fear your divine identity and its
authority in your life are under assault.
An ancient foe hopes to strip you
of this designation—don't let him.
Each day presents us with the choice
of courage or cowardice.
Choose wisely.
Wake up and be the answer
God created you to be.

THE Fight FOR

FEMALE

OTHER BOOKS BY LISA BEVERE

Without Rival

Adamant

Godmothers

Fiercely Loved

Lioness Arising

Girls with Swords

Strong

Kissed the Girls and Made Them Cry

THE

Fight

FOR

FEMALE

RECLAIMING OUR DIVINE IDENTITY

LISA BEVERE

Revell

a division of Baker Publishing Group
Grand Rapids, Michigan

Published by Revell
a division of Baker Publishing Group
Grand Rapids, Michigan
RevellBooks.com

Printed in the United States of America

Library of Congress Cataloging-in-Publication Data
Names: Bevere, Lisa, author.
Title: The fight for female : reclaiming our divine identity / Lisa Bevere.
Description: Grand Rapids, Michigan : Revell, a division of Baker Publishing Group,
    [2024] | Includes bibliographical references.
Identifiers: LCCN 2024005084 | ISBN 9780800736873 (paper) | ISBN 9780800745813
    (casebound) | ISBN 9781493445486 (ebook)
Subjects: LCSH: Women—Religious aspects—Christianity. | Self-perception—Religious
    aspects—Christianity. | Self-esteem—Religious aspects—Christianity.
Classification: LCC BT704 .B478 2024 | DDC 230.082—dc23/eng/20240222
LC record available at https://lccn.loc.gov/2024005084

Cover design by Joe Richardson

The author is represented by The FEDD Agency, Inc.

Baker Publishing Group publications use paper produced from sustainable forestry practices and postconsumer waste whenever possible.

24 25 26 27 28 29 30   7 6 5 4 3 2 1

CONTENTS

CHAPTER 1

Dreams, Dragons, and Daughters

For God speaks again and again,
though people do not recognize it.
He speaks in dreams, in visions of the night,
when deep sleep falls on people
as they lie in their beds.
He whispers in their ears
and terrifies them with warnings.

Job 33:14–16 NLT

God has spoken and God speaks. His words echo throughout the earth with divine weight and eternal purpose. The question is: *Are we listening?*

It is my urgent prayer that within my words and through the Scriptures you'll discover His voice. There is not a minute to lose. A fierce and furious dragon is loose, and he is bent on the destruction of our daughters. In the wake of our current chaos and confusion, he hopes we will forget who we are and the purpose of our womanhood.

Dreams often serve as divine messengers. They visit us in the night when the din of distraction is silenced and flee from our thoughts as we enter our day. It is only later, when something is said or seen, that we remember and think, *Why does this feel familiar? Have I been here before?*

Dreams counsel us as we sleep. Who hasn't gone to bed in one frame of mind only to wake with a completely different outlook? Then there are other dreams . . . dreams that linger until we listen. I believe that, in this day, God is whispering warnings by way of dreams.

God spoke to Joseph, the son of Jacob, through a dream that later meant provision for the children of Israel in a time of famine. God appeared to Solomon and imparted the gift of wisdom in a dream. In a dream, Joseph was told by an angel to take Mary as his wife. Another dream instructed him to flee to Egypt in order to escape a murderous king, and then another dream told him it was safe to return to Israel after Herod's death. Paul's Macedonian call came by way of a dream.

We all dream, but some dreams are nightmares. I've learned to pay attention to those as well. Especially when the nightmare is recurring. But have you ever dreamed of dragons?

I have. Nearly a decade ago.

At the time I was unsure what the dream was showing me. But I have come to believe it was a message for now. In this dream, I entered a room filled with women of all ages speaking freely with one another. These were well-educated, well-connected, and well-dressed women whose lives overflowed with feminine strength and promise. It felt as though they were known to me, yet I don't remember anyone specific. I watched from the doorway until someone turned and invited me in. But I hesitated because something was terribly amiss.

Each woman cradled a baby dragon in her arms.

These dragons were jewel-toned and outfitted in a ridiculous array of children's clothing. Ruffles and ornaments adorned their serpentine necks. I couldn't help noticing their razor-sharp teeth hovered dangerously close to the women's unprotected necks. Aghast and confused by their familiarity with the dragons, I questioned the women. "Why are you carrying a dragon? Do you understand how dangerous dragons are?"

Woman after woman smiled at my confusion. They exchanged knowing looks and shook their heads at my alarm. They drew their dragons closer as though shielding them from the foolishness of my words. They assured me these dragons were the gentle, wise variety.

But I knew different.

These dragons were not gentle or wise; they were cruel and cunning. They were predators, not pets. The dragons despised the women, but they were content to play along and lie in wait as their power grew in reach and measure.

These serpents knew I thought they were evil; they side-eyed me and I was aware of their underlying aggression. They restrained themselves because it wouldn't serve their purpose to attack or bite me. One woman encouraged me, "Pet it here where the skin is smooth."

She demonstrated how by running her finger down the curve of its neck. "See how gentle it is? Don't be afraid."

But I wasn't afraid. I was angry. Even as she spoke, I heard the dragon's reasoning in my mind. *Where would be the harm?* its silken voice goaded. *After all, petting a dragon is not the same as having one of your own.*

But I knew petting a dragon would mean partnering with its lie. Any pretense of agreement would contradict what I knew to be true. I shook my head and turned away, only to be confronted by another woman who invited me to take her dragon dressed in ruffles.

"Isn't it cute?" she cooed. "Here, hold it."

She extended her pet toward me, but rather than hold it, I reached out and snapped the dragon's neck.

The violence of my nightmare woke me.

Gone was the elegant room filled with beautiful women carrying rainbow-colored dragons. I was alone in a dark hotel room, flat on my back, arms in motion with my fists grasping at air. As a peaceful side sleeper, I felt completely disoriented by this dream that had become physical. I typed out the imagery and interactions of my dream on my iPad and lay awake until morning dawned, wondering what had just happened and what the dream meant.

There were a few things that were immediately clear, and other things that became apparent later.

First, calling dragons safe does not make them so. The things you refuse to confront when they are small have the potential to grow into something extremely threatening later. The dream was a warning. Lies are the most vulnerable to the light of truth in their inception. Partnering with lies and dragons will always prove dangerous. Adam and Eve discovered this when they agreed with the lies of a serpent. How much greater our peril if we agree with those of a dragon!

Evil is not our friend. Don't protect it, don't make excuses for it, don't partner with it, and don't hold it close. Evil has no love for humankind. Evil hates and distorts all that the Creator has fashioned. There can be no alliance between light and dark or good and evil. They are opposing forces. Do not be deceived. We were warned long ago that the dragon and his minions can masquerade as angels of light.

For even Satan disguises himself as an angel of light. (2 Cor. 11:14)

The nature of evil does not change because it is clothed in garments of innocence. And to this end, each of us should be careful what we "dress up" or make excuses for. Dragons do not belong in children's clothing.

Dragons gain power by way of theft and deception. They are agents of chaos and consumption. The only things dragons produce are more dragons. They do not create or construct anything that is useful; they use their strength solely to satisfy their appetite for devastation and destruction.

But you may be asking, *How can this be since dragons aren't real?*

There are many things that are not factual, yet they are true. Dragons are woven into the history of mankind. A very real enemy has emerged from the shadows.

He has several names: Lucifer, Satan, the father of lies, the adversary, the devil, the prince of demons, the evil one, Apollyon, Beelzebub, the deceiver, the enemy, the tempter, the prince of the power of the air, the accuser, the god of this age, the *great dragon.*

> "Fairy tales are more than true; not because they tell us that dragons exist, but because they tell us that dragons can be beaten."
>
> NEIL GAIMAN

He is bent on your destruction and the annihilation of your children. He is behind every brutal act against women. He is the author of the evil that leads to sexual assault and debasement, from kidnapping to sex trafficking. This enemy will not be placated, and if you yield an inch, he won't stop at a mile. There is no hope of a peace treaty or the option of negotiations. He is committed to stripping women of our God-given authority and distorting our feminine beauty and purpose. And yet there is hope.

Fairy tales are more than true; not because they tell us that dragons exist, but because they tell us that dragons can be beaten.

Neil Gaiman[1]

I wondered why there were no men in the room in my dream. There could be a number of reasons for this. First, I am a woman and for the most part minister to women. But even more than this, I believe that because Jesus is coming back for a bride, women and all things related to female are being specifically and strategically targeted by the enemy. He is committed to redefining and deconstructing the concept of a bride.

> "Let us rejoice and exult
>   and give him the glory,
> for the marriage of the Lamb has come,
>   and his Bride has made herself ready;
> it was granted her to clothe herself
>   with fine linen, bright and pure"—

for the fine linen is the righteous deeds of the saints. (Rev. 19:7–8)

If we are honest, there is no escaping the fact that the church looks very unlike the bride described in the book of Revelation. Tragically, we often hear of the impure and unrighteous deeds of the saints rather than the pure and righteous ones. And yet no matter how filthy we become, our Bridegroom forgives us when we repent and believes better things of us in the future.

Another curious question from the dream: How had these dragons tricked the women into believing they were pets? Snakes are rarely friends with women. One answer may be the blinding power of offense. Whenever sin is rampant in both the church and culture, an atmosphere of deception abounds (see Matt. 24). It is in this climate that men and women begin to view one another as enemies rather than as allies.

If you're even slightly paying attention, you know there is both rage at women and rage in women. With each passing day the hostility without and within becomes increasingly apparent. There is no missing that some shadowed, twisted force is seriously upset with women. There are many unholy forms that this fury adopts:

hate	distortion
rape	mutilation
abuse	pedophilia
ageism	perversion
control	accusation
cutting	gendercide
suicide	dysmorphia
poverty	minimization
racism	pornography
tension	sex trafficking
divorce	displacement
slander	cancel culture
violence	homosexuality
abortion	marginalization
silencing	sexualization of women
prejudice	misogyny (hatred of women)
eating disorders	misandry (hatred of men)

All the above and more can be summed up as the attempt to manipulate, confuse, sexualize, and erase women. But now we are aware of who is behind these attacks. Revelation 12:17 gives us a window into why:

Then the dragon became furious with the woman.

Both Scripture and Western culture view dragons as agents of death and chaos. Currently, the dragon's handiwork has destabilized our culture, and we are suffering the upheaval of divisive politics, unhealthy patriarchy, raging feminism, Marxist agenda, racism, heresy, confused gender ideologies, increased witchcraft, satanism, greed, wars, violence of all kinds, cancel and celebrity cultures, abortion, and abusive forms of religion.

These ideologies and more are used to unleash his fury. What we wrestle with is the unhuman and inhumane. His malice is woven with an evil darker than we can define.

This dragon has a systematic plan to unmake the divine imagery of male and female. He is driven by an ancient rage known as enmity, a hatred so profound that the longer it exists, the greater it grows in reach and malice. This concept of enmity is first introduced in Genesis when God addresses the serpent.

> The LORD God said to the serpent,
>
> > "Because you have done this,
> > > cursed are you above all livestock
> > > and above all beasts of the field;
> > on your belly you shall go,
> > > and dust you shall eat
> > > all the days of your life.
> > I will put enmity between you and the woman,
> > > and between your offspring and her offspring;
> > he shall bruise your head,
> > > and you shall bruise his heel." (Gen. 3:14–15)

It is important to note that God is the one who put enmity between the serpent and the woman. At the beginning of time, He positioned the woman and her seed as part of His redemptive plan and cursed the serpent and its offspring. Two legacies were forever set at odds with one another. You've heard of the term *irreconcilable differences*. It describes the parting of ways between those who were once together but cannot find a way forward. The phrase is used in divorce cases, to dissolve political affiliations, or to divide corporate entities. The parties involved agree to disagree.

Enmity is different. Enmity is irreconcilable hostility. There never was an alignment, therefore there can never be any future agreement. The only possible way for us to align is if we are deceived into mistaking our mortal enemy for a wise friend.

I believe the serpent's hope was that mankind's fall in Eden would cause us to be forever at odds with our Creator. But on the cross, Jesus closed the breach by taking our sin upon Himself. When Jesus took our place, the dragon was displaced. Now he pursues a different course.

> And when the dragon saw that he had been thrown down to the earth, he pursued the woman who had given birth to the male child. (Rev. 12:13)

What began in the garden continues to this day. He detests all that our womanhood represents. Perhaps that is the reason the ancient myths included stories of maidens sacrificed to appease dragons and abate their rage. But the dragon that threatens us will not be appeased with the lives of a few maidens.

In researching for this book, I came across a thought-provoking article, "Rescuing Our Maidens from the Culture of Death." Joseph Pearce says,

> Dragons have a preference for the virgin flesh of maidens because they are not merely hungry but wicked. They desire the defilement of the pure and undefiled, the destruction of the virgin. Their devouring is a deflowering. Parallels with human "dragons" in our own world are not difficult to discern. The war against the dragon is not, therefore, a war against a physical monster . . . but a battle against the wickedness we see around us in our everyday lives. We all face our daily dragons, and we must all defend ourselves from them and hopefully slay them, which is only possible with the assistance of God's grace. The sobering reality is that we must either fight the dragons that we encounter in life or become dragons ourselves. There is no middle path. No neutrality in this fight to the death is possible. We either fight the dragon or we become the dragon.[2]

This article was authored in 2016, the same year of my dream. Pearce also addressed the spike in suicide, sexual and physical abuse, and pornography use since 2014. If the plight of our daughters was tenuous then, it is horrific now.

Virtue is mocked as vice.

New words and prefixes are created.

Existing words are stripped of their original meaning.

Biology is subjective, and feelings are given precedence.

Marriages are contracts rather than holy covenants.

Pornography attempts online home invasions.

Preborn children are stripped of their right to life.

Gender ideologies are manipulating our children.

Women's locker rooms, bathrooms, and prisons are contested spaces.

Parents are intimidated into affirming their child's gender identity.

There's a push for pedophiles to be called "minor-attracted people."[3]

Perversion and fetishes are being normalized at an alarming rate.

And yet in some ways the spiritual battle has never been more obvious. It is not a battle *with* the souls of men and women, but a battle *for* the souls of men and women. Paul makes this distinction in Ephesians 2:1–3.

And you were dead in the trespasses and sins in which you once walked, following the course of this world, following the prince of the power of the air, **the spirit that is now at work in the sons [and daughters] of disobedience**—among whom we all once lived in the passions of our flesh, carrying out the desires of the body and the mind, and were by nature children of wrath, like the rest of mankind. (emphasis added)

We either follow the God Most High or the dragon who is "the prince of the power of the air." The dragon's spirit first ensnares, then works through, the children of disobedience.

The dragon's attack doesn't stop with us; it reaches beyond us to consume our children. When men falter, women become the last line of defense for the children. As women, we will always feel the attack on our children more intimately.

Look again at God's words to the serpent in Genesis 3:15:

> I will put enmity between you and the woman,
>> and between your offspring and her offspring;
> he shall bruise your head,
>> and you shall bruise his heel.

Most Bible scholars agree that the phrase "he shall bruise your head" refers to Jesus's triumph through the cross and the phrase "you shall bruise his heel" refers to the enemy's relentless attack on the body of Christ. We see this conflict again in Revelation 12:17:

> Then the dragon became furious with the woman and went off to make war on the rest of her offspring, on those who keep the commandments of God and hold to the testimony of Jesus.

"The woman" in this passage has plurality of meaning. She is collectively Israel, then specifically Mary; collectively the church and more exclusively the bride. What the dragon hates in its entirety he hates individually. We know the interpretation of "the woman" cannot be limited to Israel because they (literal Israel) do not currently hold to the testimony of Jesus.

This fight for female is not a fight for women's rights—it is a battle to rescue and recover our divine birthright. What one generation forfeits, the next fights to recover. There are battles for the men to fight and there are battles only women can win. This is our fight and it will require repentance, redemption, and rescue. I believe we are poised for the restoration and recovery of what has been misplaced, displaced, and stolen from our feminine identity for decades.

This fight for female is not a fight for women's rights—it is a battle to rescue and recover our divine birthright.

For too long we've battled one another, blinded to our true enemy. We've exhausted ourselves fighting the wrong battles and wrestling allies. It is time to speak words of hope and life rather than words of death and despair. It is not too late for us to remember who we truly are. We are the dragon's enemy.

Heavenly Father,

I come to You in the name of Jesus. I believe I was born for this moment that is at once terrifying and wondrous. Thank You for entrusting me with the honor of being a female. Show me how You see the wonder and the beauty of this fight to recover what has been lost.

CHAPTER 2

The Fight for Divine Identity

> *So God created man in his own image,*
> *in the image of God he created him;*
> *male and female he created them.*
>
> *Genesis 1:27*

More than two decades ago, I realized I was not who I said I was.

When I got married more than forty years ago, I neglected to legally change my name. I was under the mistaken impression that when I surrendered my Indiana driver's license with my maiden name on it and put Bevere on my new Texas license, everything was taken care of. From that day forward, Bevere was the only name I used. Every check I signed, every paycheck I received, any book I authored was under my new surname. When we moved to Florida, I turned in my Texas license under the same assumption. Everything was fine until I went to the DMV for my Colorado license.

After an excessively long wait, my name was called. But when I got to the counter, they refused to issue a license because, according to their records, Lisa Bevere didn't exist. A trip to the DMV is challenging on the best of days, but this became the worst. I showed them my passport that had my maiden and married names hyphenated. I assured them there was a mistake. But as far as the DMV was concerned, I didn't exist under either name. Frantic, I explained I'd written books, paid taxes, and been employed under that very name. I handed the woman my Florida license with Bevere as my surname. But to no avail because, according to their records, neither name belonged to me.

I stepped aside and burst into tears.

Moved with compassion, the clerk volunteered, "If you can prove that's your maiden name, we will give you a license."

How would I do that? I exited the DMV, took a deep breath, and called the registrar's office at the university I'd attended. They were kind enough to fax me documents that proved my identity.

As stressful as my trip to the DMV turned out to be, it could have been worse. What if I'd forgotten who I was? What if I believed them when they said neither name belonged to me? I would have accepted the loss of my name. But I knew who I was, so that was never going to happen. It didn't matter that they didn't know who I was because I never doubted my identity.

I couldn't prove who I was by what I had done or with the license I carried. They wanted to know my name of origin. They wanted me to prove I was my father's child. Life without an innate awareness of who we really are could be likened to navigating the uncharted wild without a compass. And yet we are living in a time when the female identity is being brought into question.

Before I even shared my dragon dream, you probably knew something was amiss. It may be the very reason you are hearing my words. At first the dragon's shadow was an undercurrent, a few additions to our language, a slight alteration to what we've known as women. Then it became more than words and various ideologies; it has grown into a war on females with the meaning of womanhood under siege.

Perhaps you feel it is too extreme to label it a war. That my terminology is too harsh or fatalistic. If so, I understand. But while we have hesitated and carefully measured our words, the dragon has escalated his assault against our children.

This book has easily been the most difficult I've written . . . ever. I've wrestled with words until I'm exhausted. I have never experienced so much spiritual warfare or so many physical challenges. I have found myself pulled between anger and heartbreak. I've written on identity before, but never has the message been more urgent. It is not enough to know *who* you are; it's essential you know *why* before it is too late.

I'm watching as the image and meaning of *female* and *woman* are being systematically downgraded or reduced. The enemy wants to pervert the image of female because female was created in the image of God.

We desecrate the image of God at our own peril.

Perhaps we've been careless because we haven't understood what it means to bear His image. The word *image* is first used in Genesis 1:26:

Then God said, "Let us make man in our image, after our likeness."

The word *image* here expresses an idea, vision, reflection, or concept in the imagination—as well as a divine representation—of your Creator. This means you are God's idea.

Both male and female are uniquely created to reflect His image. Just because woman was the last to be created, do not imagine this makes her the least. Female was always part of God's divine vision. The very concept of woman illustrates our Creator's profound care and response to our longings. Both the feminine and masculine are captured in the term *imago Dei*. This in and of itself is an incomparable entrustment.

In light of this, Genesis 1:27 should challenge our self-perception. Rather than bowing to the limits of self, or how we see ourselves, the *image of God* is a revelation of how God sees us. *Female* has always had divine identity and purpose. But the dragon wants to strip humanity of any divine connection by encouraging us to worship what is less. Romans 1:21 tells us,

> For although they knew God, they did not honor him as God or give thanks to him, but they became futile in their thinking, and their foolish hearts were darkened.

When God is not honored as God, our minds are overrun with futility and our hearts are blackened by foolishness. Our history from Eden to the cross is a litany of failures after the fall: there was a flood, a tower, idolatry in the desert, then idolatry in the promised land, all of which led to wars and exiles. When God's image bearers weren't sinning by worshiping the lesser, we were busy twisting worship into a collection of relentless religious rules. Each desecration distorted our semblance of His divine imagery. Humanity had lost its way; we became lifeless, hopeless, as we struggled in an oppressive, desperate world torn by division. Because we lost our way, we behaved in cruel and inhumane ways.

God heard our anguish and responded with a divine rescue. Rather than reject and push us away after millennia of rebellion, God drew closer and ransomed His wayward image bearers with the life of His only begotten Son. Why? Because of His love for us. He knew we'd all need the love of a Father and a family to call our own. In Christ, He adopted us and called us sons and daughters.

> See what kind of love the Father has given to us, that we should be called children of God; and so we are. The reason why the world does not know us is that it did not know him. (1 John 3:1)

The depth of this gift is evidenced by what He calls us, His children. All humanity was created to reflect the image of God, but only children reflect their Father's nature. Everyone is an image bearer, but not everyone is a child of God. We have become His. The passage in 1 John continues,

> Beloved, we are God's children now, and what we will be has not yet appeared; but we know that when he appears we shall be like him, because we shall see him as he is. And everyone who thus hopes in him purifies himself as he is pure. (vv. 2–3)

In Scripture, there is both the promise of *now* and the promise of *what will be*; we are children who reflect God's heart and nature. Our hope is in Him, and as we pursue God, He reveals, refines, restores, and transforms us.

When we come to faith there is a great exchange. Jesus Christ purchased our complete freedom so that we could be completely His. We are invited to surrender our broken, sin-filled, self-focused, sensual nothingness for His glorious everything. We exchange our dead temporal life for His eternal life, our self-will is surrendered for His divine will, our brokenness is replaced with His healing love, and our thoughts and ways are first surrendered then raised to His. He loved us long before we knew Him and chose us long before we knew we had a choice. Under the lordship of Jesus, the domination of sin and darkness is over. We no longer follow the dictates of self—we follow the lead of our Savior King, and the Holy Spirit is our Counselor and Guide. God is your Father, and you are a daughter of the God Most High.

Daughter

You are divinely sealed by the One who identified you as His own.
Your identity is daughter.
My identity is daughter.

Your heavenly Father is more committed to you than you can imagine.

You were adopted long before you were abandoned.

You were rescued long before you were lost.

You were foreknown and predestined to be His.

The designation of *daughter* . . .

Is far more intimate than girl or woman.

Brings more wholeness than marriage.

Is the embrace of family.

Declares *wanted* and *welcome*.

Tells the world *you belong*.

Acknowledges that you are *fathered*.

Whispers *mothered*.

Daughter is a declaration of protection and provision.

Daughters are loved. This is true regardless of how your life began, and it is true no matter how difficult or confusing your life may now be. Know this: you were always wanted.

I've had the honor of holding many roles in my life: wife, mother, grandmother, mother-in-law, author, and minister. Each is an aspect of my life, but they are not me. Our world or culture identifies us by our achievements and responsibilities, but these are functions or roles, they are not our identity. Roles and résumés describe what we do; our identity tells the story of who we are and who we are related to. What I have, what I wear, where I live, what I drive are possessions. At any given time, all of these can change or be lost. If it can be taken from you, then it is peripheral to your identity. Which is why no one should ever allow their possessions to define them. Only God has the right of bestowing identity. You are not what you do; you are what was done for you.

We need the grounding of our divine identity in days fraught with chaos and confusion. You were first fashioned to reflect the image of God and then redeemed to be His daughter. The Creator of all that is, seen and unseen, created you. He sees you, loves you, and I would go as far as to say needs you to believe that you were woven on purpose for a divine purpose.

> You are more than what you do and more than what you've done.
> You are more than what you own and more than who you know.
> You are more than what you see and what you choose to show others.
> You are more known than you could possibly understand.
> More loved than you can imagine.
> Your identity is a divine gift.

Your divine identity includes your body, but it is not limited to your body, because you are obviously more than your body.

Your divine identity includes your soul, but it is more than your soul, because you are also body and spirit.

Your divine identity includes your spirit, but it is not limited to your spirit, because we are triune beings that include body, soul, and spirit.

Our body is our framework, the soul is our mind, will, and emotions, and our spirit is the breath of God. These three are intimately intertwined, and sacred. As Ecclesiastes reminds us, "A threefold cord is not quickly broken" (4:12).

You may not feel that every part of you is sacred. You may feel that scarred, flawed, and imperfect would be a more accurate description. Your Creator sees more than brokenness in your framework. You may describe your soul as dysfunctional, triggered, frightened, or even angry. God sees your soul clothed in His righteousness. You may believe your spirit was made new when you were born again but still imagine *sacred* to be a stretch. It is the very reason why God gave us His holiness rather than our own—and invites us into a lifelong journey of transformation in Him.

What We Reflect

Even though our vision is currently limited, shadowed, and separated by time and space, a day is coming when we will be fully alive and know God fully. Paul reminds us,

> For now we see in a mirror dimly, but then face to face. Now I know in part; then I shall know fully, even as I have been fully known. (1 Cor. 13:12)

We may be dim-sighted now, but I assure you that our heavenly Father is not. Right now, you are fully known and fully loved. And each of us has a desperate human longing for both. We live in a day of almost limitless access to one another, and yet never has there been a time when so many have felt misunderstood, desperately unknown, and unseen. Even when there is a spark or moment of popularity, a few minutes of "fame," we cannot help but wonder if we were seen or if it was a facade we projected in the hope that we'd be loved and accepted.

When you look in a mirror, what do you see?

Do you see a soul wracked by failures and disappointments?

Do you see a body that is disappointing, or worse—a mistake?

Do you see a life powered by the Spirit or one ruled by the limits of self-consciousness? A reflected image cannot reveal more than it is shown. And like a mirror, it cannot show what it does not see.

God wants to be the image we behold, then the image we reflect. When we do this, He invites us into a life of divine appointments. As Psalm 34:5 reminds us, "Those who look to him are radiant, and their faces shall never be ashamed."

In preparation for this book, I've drawn on science, history, literature, and Scripture. I've listened to podcasts, newscasts, and arguments. I started and stopped writing so many times that each chapter felt like yet another puzzle piece needing to be flipped to discover its placement. My hope is that together we can find the borders and reassemble the beautiful imagery of female for our sake—and the sake of our sons and daughters.

Earlier I spoke of the threefold cord that makes up your divine identity: body, soul, and spirit. I want you to see these facets of your life as divinely woven cords that are interdependent and intimately connected with one another. I like to think of these strands as unity, strength, and faith. If this is accurate, we have unity in the spirit, strength in our body, and the gift of faith for our soul.

These are activated when we have a Christ-consciousness that overrides the messages of self-consciousness that limit us with insecurity, comparison, and pride. Self-rule will inevitably steer us in the direction of being self-centered, self-confident, self-conscious, self-motivated, self-identified, self-serving, self-righteous, and self-sabotaging, and eventually toward living a selfish life. Self-image is tied to our appearance, conversations, achievements, education, relationships, and possessions. If we become too busy curating a projected image, we lose touch with our truest identity of daughters created in the image of God.

Time and distance have a way of eroding an awareness of our divine origin. And yet when we pause, we sense something is amiss. In the silence, we hear a whisper, an invitation: *You were created for more.* A glorious hope. An eternal mindset. God wired us with an innate knowing that there is more than this life. More than things. More than our bodies. More than our achievements. This longing invites us to lift our gaze. Colossians 3:2 admonishes us,

> Set your minds on things that are above, not on things that are on earth.

We wrestle when we have the wrong mindset. We struggle when we look in the wrong places for this divine "more." Rather than search the heavens for the imprint of our Creator, we settle for lowering our gaze to the realm of self. We settle for less when we are disappointed in people, disappointed in government and organizations, disappointed with religion, and disappointed in ourselves. But no matter how we try to reorient ourselves, actualize ourselves, or simply conform to the limits of self, the weight of divine gravity is upon us.

As a female, you are *uniquely empowered* by God to carry out His purposes. Image bearer was your beginning; daughter of God is your destiny. It's time to fight for your divine identity.

———

At the ends of chapters 2–12, I've included questions to help you think about what this fight for female might look like in your life. I hope you'll take time to think, pray, and write your ideas.

How have you been referring to or identifying yourself? Do you find yourself saying, "I'm just _____"?

What comes to mind when you hear "daughter of God"?

What is one area where you are self-ruled or self-reliant that you could surrender or exchange for Christ reliance?

CHAPTER 3

The Fight for Your Sacred Space

For we do not have a high priest who is unable to sympathize with our weaknesses, but one who in every respect has been tempted as we are, yet without sin.

Hebrews 4:15

Have you ever wondered if Jesus understands the discomfort of being female? Or maybe your question runs deeper. Does Jesus understand how uncomfortable you are as a woman?

As I sought to understand the struggle and even the pain of those who are incredibly uncomfortable in their bodies, I turned to the Scriptures and discovered my answers.

First, Jesus may have been more uncomfortable in His human form than any of us have the capacity to realize. Philippians tells us,

Have this mind among yourselves, which is yours in Christ Jesus, who, though he was in the form of God, did not count equality with God a thing to be grasped, but emptied himself, by taking the form of a servant, being born in the likeness of men. (2:5–7)

He gets us because He became us.

Imagine this if you can: Jesus laid aside His divine privileges and form and limited Himself to the confines and constraints of our human flesh. He chose to be uncomfortable so that in Him we would find comfort.

And if a house is divided against itself, that house will not be able to stand. (Mark 3:25)

I know this verse addresses spiritual kingdoms, but division diminishes the strength of things that were once united. How many women live as divided houses when it comes to our feminine form? We criticize and curse our bodies rather than celebrate and bless them. Instead of enjoying the individual uniqueness and abilities of our bodies, we have a love-hate relationship with our shapes. Before long we find ourselves inhabiting divided spaces or we feel imprisoned in despised houses. And what we say to ourselves has the power to affect our bodies all the way down to the cellular level. Science is proving that "death and life are in the power of the tongue" (Prov. 18:21). In their book *Words Can Change Your Brain*, Dr. Andrew Newberg and Mark Robert Waldman write, "A single word has the power to influence the expression of genes that regulate physical and emotional stress."[1]

I remember the day my soul and body fractured and I became a divided house. I walked in from school and discovered that my father was home early and both my mother and brother were out. My father was an intimidating figure of a man. I greeted him and headed directly to my room to do homework, but he called me back to our family room. I sensed something different in his tone. Was it disappointment? My mind raced. Had I done something wrong?

"Come here," he grumbled.

I approached the black leather chair where my father sat smoking.

"Turn around." He motioned, cigarette in hand.

I obliged with an awkward 360.

He let out an audible sigh and shook his head. "Lisa, how much do you weigh? Your butt is huge!"

I froze. I had absolutely no idea. I hadn't been weighed since summer camp. I volunteered my camp weight.

My father countered, "Well, you're not at camp anymore. Go weigh yourself and come back here."

Weigh myself? Was that a thing?

Until that day, I'd only been weighed for physicals. I trekked down the hall to my parents' master bathroom. I flipped on the lights and hesitantly stepped on their scale. I stepped off to confirm it was zeroed. It was. My dad was right; I'd gained nearly twenty pounds since camp. Ashamed, I slunk back to my father and reported my weight. He folded his paper, laid it aside, transferred his cigarette to the ashtray, and invited me to sit down. I leaned in for what I knew was about to be a serious talk.

"Lisa, that's too much. You're fat. No one will want to date you. You need to take care of it."

I nodded and that was it. He picked up his cigarette and paper and I was dismissed.

As I walked to my room, I wondered, how had I missed this? Did other people think I was fat? Was that why the guy I didn't even like broke up with me? I locked the door to my room, pulled down the blinds, and quickly stripped down to my bra and underwear. I climbed atop my bed so I could see my body's reflection in the dresser mirror. I was horrified by what I saw. How had this happened? I hated my headless reflection, scored with creases about my waist and the impressions of seams up and down my thighs from jeans that had grown too tight. In that moment my body became an enemy. I spoke hateful words and threatened the puffy image in the mirror. I became a house divided.

At dinner, I ate half my normal amount of food under the watchful eye of my father. After dinner, I donned my swim team sweats and ran in the snow until my lungs ached. I began sneaking my mother's fashion magazines into my bedroom. Perhaps these impossibly beautiful women on shiny pages held the answer to my body's dilemma. But rather than provide comfort or counsel, their svelte bodies and flawless faces mocked me. I became their willing disciple, ready to try any fad diet or exercise they presented, and I was rewarded. The weight fell off. My father affirmed my efforts. Suddenly, I was noticed. Guys asked me out. Then I drew some unhealthy parallels:

Thin women are worthy of love and attention.
Thin women are in control of their lives.
Thin women are successful.

I was fifteen.

The breach that began that day widened until my weight controlled my life in college. It was seven years of crazy before I experienced healing at the age of twenty-two. If this was my reaction to a one-time, one-on-one encounter, imagine what our daughters and other young women are fighting now!

The imagery has moved beyond still photos on shiny paper. The images women fight are alive, and there is no escaping them because they are in our hands. Each day, filtered images speak to us, reminding us of what we lack. I am not against using filters; I've used them myself in bad lighting or on partial makeup days. What I am against is the unreal expectations they put on us. I remember when Instagram was a way to keep up with friends and encourage others. Now it is a realm where we compare ourselves to everyone.

Abigail Shrier's groundbreaking book *Irreversible Damage* exposed the inherent dangers tied to a constant diet of comparison and distorted gender ideologies.

Nearly every novel problem teenagers face traces itself back to 2007 and the introduction of Steve Jobs's iPhone. In fact, the explosion in self-harm can be so precisely pinpointed to the introduction of this one device that researchers have little doubt that it is the cause. . . . The statistical explosion of bullying, cutting, anorexia, depression, and the rise of sudden transgender identification is owed to the self-harm instruction, manipulation, abuse, and relentless harassment supplied by a single smartphone.[2]

And these problems have only worsened since her book was released. Many of these trends have reached epidemic proportions. And Christian women are far from exempt. They experience the same struggles, often layered with a large side of religious shame. It is unlikely that you will defend or celebrate something you've been told is sinful or carnal. But a woman's body is neither.

Not Second Best

Female is not an afterthought, second choice, or downgrade. Female was creation's finale. Jesus refers to the church as His beloved bride. Men are not more redeemed than women. Galatians 3:28 tells us,

There is neither Jew nor Greek, there is neither slave nor free, there is no male and female, for you are all one in Christ Jesus.

Jesus has made all things new and healed the breach between male and female by making us all one. But to be clear, *one* does not mean "the same." And just as you are not an afterthought, your female body is not an afterthought.

Female is not an afterthought, second choice, or downgrade. Female was creation's finale.

Our female bodies are divinely aligned to glorify God. Yet the enemy of our souls is also the enemy of our bodies. He distorts the imagery of our body's form because he hates the potential of our body's function. He loves to simultaneously sexualize and shame the feminine form. And on some level, our silence has allowed this downgrade of our female form by our current culture. In other ways we've been participants. If we stopped buying the products, singing the songs, and wearing the clothes that diminish our divine image, things would shift. Perhaps we've allowed this to happen because we forgot that our bodies are sacred and imagined seduction was our only option.

> I praise you because I am fearfully and wonderfully made;
> your works are wonderful,
> I know that full well. (Ps. 139:14 NIV)

Have you *really* pondered this revelation? I need you to sit with this one for a while to grasp what it means to know the wonder of your body "full well." Both the male and female bodies are uniquely woven and holy. In my experience as a mother to four sons and mother-in-law to four daughters, this realization comes easier for men. They rarely question the wonder of their bodies. Women are far more critical of their bodies and find any revelation of wonder more difficult to embrace. Tragically, both cultural confusion and religious distortions have provided women with countless reasons to believe otherwise. It is okay to wrestle with questions if we don't allow those queries to cause us to question His love.

Let's explore this concept on a deeper, more personal feminine level. The psalmist had no problem recognizing God's creative handiwork reflected within himself. The Message frames David's words in Psalm 139:14 this way:

> Oh yes, you shaped me first inside, then out;
>   you formed me in my mother's womb.
> I thank you, High God—you're breathtaking!
>   Body and soul, I am marvelously made!
> I worship in adoration—what a creation!

Do you believe this? That you were purposefully and intricately shaped by God from the inside out? I hope so. And yet, we most often measure ourselves in the reverse, from the outside in. Hear this: You were loved and wanted when your presence was but a flutter, or a whisper, a mere shadow of what your life is now. You were loved and longed for in the sanctuary of your mother's womb. Yes. Even if your mother didn't want you, your Father was masterfully weaving together your body and soul. Sadly, women disassociate their soul from their body, and wrongly imagine it is only the human soul that God loves. But that is a lie. This lie has contributed to our current state of bodily confusion. This mindset of loving one and despising the other chisels away at the intimate body and soul connection. The enemy loves to exploit this fissure.

Maybe when you've read this psalm in the past, you've mentally pushed it aside. You reason it is a verse meant for men. Or if you dared to believe that this revelation of wonder was for you . . . you saw it as a delayed promise, a one-day, someday thing. One day when you lose weight, exercise regularly, and fit into your pre-pregnancy clothes (feel free to insert your personal disqualifiers here), then you'll embrace these words as your own. But for now, the concept of *full well* escapes your grasp. I dare you to embrace it now—if not for yourself, do it for the sake of your daughters.

I am sad that many women believe God was not intimately involved in their creation. They imagine their frame to be misaligned or a misshapen fit. For some, the pain runs deeper. They loathe their female body. They do not see wonder; they only see vulnerabilities and limitations. Maybe someone trespassed your frame, and now your body and soul feel fractured. There are many reasons your body might feel like a prison you long to escape. All of which our Lord understands. Please know you are not alone in your struggle, and even though I never wrestled with gender dysphoria, for quite a while I certainly wasn't happy that I'd been born a girl. Even more so after becoming a Christian.

If you escape the snare of sin, the enemy will seek to trap you in the bondage of religion. The dragon wants us jumping from one pit to the other in an attempt to bind us in the very realms Jesus died to set us free from. He wants us mastered by our flesh or our flesh mastered by legalism. He doesn't want us to be free daughters of the Spirit; he wants to entrap us with the passions or shortcomings of our flesh. For many years I cried out in anguish until I experienced the unique, tender expression of love God reserves for His daughters and Jesus's intimate wooing of His bride. Beautiful daughter, be at peace. Your Creator wants to bring you back to a place of freedom and wholeness.

Let's look at ourselves again with fresh eyes. Lay aside all the imagery and voices that stream and scream perpetual comparison. The very ones that always remind you of what you are not. Constantly broadcasting, *Do this, buy that, because you're not thin enough, strong enough, young enough, pretty enough, pursued enough, desirable enough, rich enough, on trend or sexy enough.*

And no, I'm not going to say that you're more than enough, but I am going to say that you are worthy of wonder and worthy of His love. Not because of anything you have done but because of what He has done.

Fearfully and wonderfully made is not about our image or our feelings. It has nothing to do with where we live, what we drive, or what we own. We are fearfully, wonderfully, and uniquely

THE FIGHT FOR YOUR SACRED SPACE

loved as women. We are without rival because we are fathered by the God Most High, the heirs of the One without equal. We are daughters beyond compare. Your body is His workmanship. I understand that you may not feel this way about yourself on any given day, at any given age, or in any given situation or season of life. Psalm 139 is not about your feelings; it is how your Creator made and feels about you.

> You are loved. Here and now loved. Not someday loved, you are now loved. His love is what makes us holy and whole.

You are loved. Here and now loved. Not someday loved, you are now loved. His love is what makes us holy and whole.

Created with Intention

Your body is the wonderful work of an intentional Creator. David reveled in the wonder of God's achievement. He lived in a continuous revelation of creation and his Creator's wonder. For most of us, it stops there. We see the wonder in the stars, the mountains, the ocean, and nature. We see wonder in children. You glimpse wonder in your friends. But do you see that wonder in an unfiltered version of you? We, both male and female, were created in the image of God, then became the children of God. Please allow this to sink in. We began as a reflection and now we are His offspring. We were created by Him for Him.

> I appeal to you therefore, brothers, by the mercies of God, to present your bodies as a living sacrifice, holy and acceptable to God, which is your spiritual worship. (Rom. 12:1)

In the past, I've emphasized the concept of a living sacrifice to the neglect of the reality that in Christ my form is holy and acceptable. The NIV says "holy and pleasing." Through the cross, exchanges were made, the unholy became holy, the formerly rejected became the accepted, and those alienated from the life of God became partakers of His divine nature. He died for us so that we might live for Him, not in part but in whole.

His death made us alive. Our obedience allows what Jesus did to gain expression in and through our lives. His sacrifice made us sacred. But if I despise my body, how can it ever be a vehicle of worship? If God calls my body holy and acceptable, who am I to call it wholly unacceptable? Changing how we view our bodies begins by renewing our minds.

> Do not conform to the pattern of this world, but be transformed by the renewing of your mind. Then you will be able to test and approve what God's will is—his good, pleasing and perfect will. (Rom. 12:2 NIV)

Renewing our minds means looking at every aspect of our life as God-formed and wonderful. Where there is a lack of wonder, there is an environment of lack. A lack of curiosity, joy, care, strength, and time. My four greatest moments of wonder were when my sons were born. I had never felt more empowered than after I gave birth. I was awed by the wonder of my body and by each little life I held in my arms, and so was my husband. It could possibly be argued that women are even more fearfully and wonderfully made than men. David was a warrior who took thousands of lives, but he never brought forth a life. Women are warriors for life.

Rather than wasting time worrying about what we are not, let's invite God into every area of our life that now is. N. T. Wright's commentary on these passages helps us make this connection:

> For Paul, the mind and the body are closely interconnected, and must work as a coherent team. Having one's mind renewed

and offering God one's body (verse 1) are all part of the same complete event. Here Paul uses a vivid, indeed shocking, idea: one's whole self (that's what Paul means by "body") must be laid on the altar like a sacrifice in the Temple. The big difference is that, whereas the sacrifice is there to be killed, the Christian's self-offering is actually all about coming alive with the new life that bursts out in unexpected ways once the evil deeds of the self are put to death.[3]

Why not let His life within us burst out and touch the lives of others in unexpected ways?

He Is the Answer to the Hard Questions

Not long ago, a beautiful woman and friend asked me a heartfelt question, "What would Jesus say to my friend who believes she was born in the wrong body?"

I took a deep breath before answering her. Then I said, "I believe first He would affirm His love for her."

My friend nodded. And I continued, "I also believe He'd tell her, 'You're not a mistake. But I understand your discomfort.' Then He would explain that this world is not her home and that she'd never feel completely comfortable here because she was made for eternity."

We long for more because we were made for more. We fight aging and death because we were made for eternal life. As wondrous as our bodies are, they are merely the seed form of what they one day will be. Paul explained it this way in 1 Corinthians 15:42–44:

> So is it with the resurrection of the dead. What is sown is perishable; what is raised is imperishable. It is sown in dishonor; it is raised in glory. It is sown in weakness; it is raised in power. It is sown a natural body; it is raised a spiritual body. If there is a natural body, there is also a spiritual body.

You might think of it this way: If you'd never seen a tomato or tomato plant, could you imagine either of them simply by looking at a small, oddly shaped, colorless tomato seed? That tiny seed would have no way of telling you what was within it. And yet, given the right environment, that tomato seed will explode with growth in color and flavor. We are the same. In this moment, we are merely seeds waiting for the right environment to reveal what we one day will be. Paul goes on to say,

> Thus it is written, "The first man Adam became a living being"; the last Adam [Jesus] became a life-giving spirit. But it is not the spiritual that is first but the natural, and then the spiritual. The first man was from the earth, a man of dust; the second man is from heaven. (vv. 45–47)

For now, we are dust and seeds, born of earth and born again to be reborn in heaven. Why would any of us think our dust-and-seed state would be comfortable when we sense there is so much more waiting within us? We are in a state of agitated containment. We are in the tension of who we are and who we will forever be. The seed of our "more" will not be realized until His appearance.

But the dragon lies and says, *This life is all there will ever be. Be your own god.* The enemy wants a generation of sons and daughters to imagine *their formation was a mistake.* If he can get them to believe this lie, how will they ever trust a mistaken Creator with the weightier measure of their transformation? By twisting the truth, the enemy wants us to doubt the One who is the truth. C. S. Lewis wrote,

> A creature revolting against a creator is revolting against the source of his own powers—including even his power to revolt. . . . It is like the scent of a flower trying to destroy the flower.[4]

To understand this Lewis quote in its deepest sense, our role in this statement requires more clarity. We are the creature, not the Creator, and as such, we fall into the category of those who are empowered rather than the One who is all Power. We are the scent, the fragrant vapor of a blossom, but not the flower.

This comparison captures the disparity between the One who creates magnificence out of nothingness and those He created. Think of it: without His gift of free will, even rebellion would be impossible. And yet we still revolt and find ourselves blinded to reason. The prophet Isaiah described our frailty this way:

> A voice says, "Cry!"
>   And I said, "What shall I cry?"
> All flesh is grass,
>   and all its beauty is like the flower of the field.
> The grass withers, the flower fades
>   when the breath of the LORD blows on it;
>   surely the people are grass.
> The grass withers, the flower fades,
>   but the word of our God will stand forever. (Isa. 40:6–8)

The breath of God's Word cannot fade. James echoed the brevity of our days with this insight:

> What is your life? For you are a mist that appears for a little time and then vanishes. (James 4:14)

In light of eternity, we are a fleeting fragrance, a scent that disappears only to reappear in eternity. The words of C. S. Lewis reflect the ancient laments of the prophet Isaiah.

> You turn things upside down!
> Shall the potter be regarded as the clay,
> that the thing made should say of its maker,
>   "He did not make me";
> or the thing formed say of him who formed it,
>   "He has no understanding"? (Isa. 29:16)

In so many ways and on so many fronts, our worldview has turned the vantage of the sacred upside down. Does clay tell the artisan, "You didn't make me," or say to the maker, "You didn't know what you were doing"? Isaiah is my favorite prophet, but he has taken the gloves off in these verses! Through him, the Lord is exposing the breakdown between the created and the Creator. Paraphrased, it might read, "You are the ones in My hands. I am not in yours." We are His idea. I fear we've embraced this flipped reasoning once again. In Isaiah 45:9 the prophet addresses the issue again:

> Woe to him who strives with him who formed him,
>   a pot among earthen pots!
> Does the clay say to him who forms it, "What are you
>   making?"
> or "Your work has no handles"?

The word *woe* should serve as a "whoa" for all of us! It is time to stop and return to reason.

In her excellent book *Love Thy Body*, Nancy Pearcey comments on this same idea:

> Why is it considered acceptable to carve up a person's body to match their inner sense of self but bigoted to help them change their sense of self to match their body? Feelings can change. But the body is an observable fact that does not change. It makes sense to treat it as a reliable marker of sexual identity.[5]

This is an important question for us to answer. Is it not striving with our Maker when we demand that our feelings and our self-perception take precedence over His divine formation? Do we want to further the destruction of division by separating gender from our biological sex? Yes, there are very real challenges to be faced in our highly sexualized, invasive world. Yes, we should love people no matter what they choose to do to their body. Yes, God loves people no matter what decisions they make. But don't you see the dragon's shadow behind this?

He whispers lies: *Life will be better, you will be safer, you will be loved if you change.* What he does not want you to know is that life is not easy; it

> You will never be safer than when Christ is your refuge.

is eternal. You don't have to change to be loved; you are already loved, and you will never be safer than when Christ is your refuge.

He sees us as we one day will be, transformed and completely renewed.

I am a flawed, imperfect mother and grandmother, yet my heart still leaps whenever I see my children or grandchildren. I love them. I want the best for them. I see the best in them. If I feel this way, how much more does our heavenly Father, who is love?

———

In what ways have you lived as a house divided?

What part of your female frame do you shame?

Can you pinpoint a moment when this division happened?

What is one thing you can do to reconnect with your body, to see it as a sacred space created by God?

CHAPTER 4

The Fight in the Spirit Realm

When an enemy wants nothing but your defeat and annihilation, neutrality means choosing death.

Dr. Michael Heiser

The demonic realm is real. What we are wrestling in the natural realm will be won in the spiritual realm.

Before John and I married, I returned home for a few months to prepare for our wedding, but the oppression in my parents' house was overwhelming. The atmosphere of the house felt permeated by a sense of hopelessness. There were nights I'd wake suddenly from a deep sleep with an unseen presence pushing me down into my bed. I felt choked when I tried to call on the name of Jesus. I'd hear, *Quiet, you can't speak that name. You're unworthy.*

But I knew it was a lie. The moment I whispered, *"Jesus!"* every trace of the evil fled. There is undeniable authority in the name of Jesus. And believers don't have to earn the right to use His name; it was given freely to those who know Him.

> Behold, I have given you authority to tread on serpents and scorpions, and over all the power of the enemy, and nothing shall hurt you. (Luke 10:19)

The emphasis here is on our God-given authority rather than encounters with evil. There's no need for snake handling or dancing on scorpions when evil might be as close as the phone in your hand. To fight against evil, we must know the Word and walk in the authority of the Holy Spirit. The Holy Spirit is Lord over the gifts of the Spirit. First Corinthians 12:7–11 tells us,

> A spiritual gift is given to each of us so we can help each other. To one person the Spirit gives the ability to give **wise advice**; to another the same Spirit gives a message of **special knowledge**. The same Spirit gives **great faith** to another, and to someone else the one Spirit gives **the gift of healing**. He gives one person **the power to perform miracles**, and another **the ability to prophesy**. He gives someone else **the ability to discern whether a message is from the Spirit of God or from another spirit**. Still another person is given **the ability to speak in unknown languages**, while another is given **the ability to interpret what is being said**. It is the one and only Spirit who distributes all these gifts. He alone decides which gift each person should have. (NLT, emphasis added)

I want to highlight a few things. First, we each have a spiritual gift. Next, the reason for the gift is to help others. If it is not helpful to other people, it's probably not from the Holy Spirit. I boldfaced some of these gifts of the Spirit: wise advice, special knowledge, or insight, great faith, the gift of healing, power to perform miracles, the ability to prophesy, the ability to discern what is of God's Spirit or another spirit, the ability to speak unknown languages, and the ability to interpret those languages. That's the list.

Answer me honestly, would any of these gifts be helpful today? I certainly think so! We all could use a bit more of most of these in our lives. We desperately need wisdom, special knowledge, and healing! These three would be amazing. I do see some people operating in their giftings, but we need to see more people empowered by the Holy Spirit. And these gifts shouldn't only be platformed in meetings; they should be put into practice and outworked in our daily lives. Everywhere you go, people are in need of encouragement and direction.

I think the problem arises when the church emphasizes the gift rather than its purpose. I understand many churches may not teach on these gifts or train people how to steward the gift to serve other believers. But people who have faithfully stewarded their gift have been difference makers in my life. I challenge you to pray and ask God what gift the Holy Spirit has for you so you can help others. Then pray and receive it.

A Discerning Spirit

The seventh year of our marriage was an extremely tense season. John was serving as the college and career pastor at a church, but someone in leadership wanted him gone. It felt like every week he was on the verge of being fired. We had two small children, and I found myself under an enormous amount of stress. I would question John: "Aren't you concerned about your job?"

But John refused to be caught up in my whirlwind of worry. And I was worrying enough for both of us. Why was my husband in trouble? We had a discipleship group within our youth group whom we asked to read their Bibles, pray daily, and stay away from R-rated movies. And one of the parents with the power to fire John didn't like it.

One night when things were at their worst, I woke from a deep sleep. I thought our infant son had stirred. I slipped out of bed to check on him, but he was sleeping soundly in his cradle. It was the middle of the night, but I felt strangely alert and sensed a call to prayer.

I entered our moonlit family room. I circled the room, praying quietly as I felt led by the Spirit. It wasn't long before my prayers became impassioned. I was tired of this attack on our family, but I was unsure what we were up against. I asked the Holy Spirit to give me insight and continued to pray and pace the room. I sensed the atmosphere shift and felt I wasn't alone. I opened my eyes and discovered an apparition of a giant woman in our two-story foyer. She looked like a hologram that was a cross between Cleopatra and an Amazon. She was fiercely beautiful and strong but angry. Even so, in the moment I felt no fear. She didn't move or speak; I was seeing a revelation of what we were battling, the discerning of spirits (see 1 Cor. 12:10). I spoke the name that came to me.

"It's Jezebel," I whispered. "We are fighting a Jezebel spirit."

We were at war with a ruling spirit that hates repentance. I continued to walk and pray until I felt a release. When I looked again, the image was gone and I was alone. I climbed back into bed and fell asleep.

The next morning, as I reflected on what had happened the night before, I sensed the Holy Spirit saying, *Renounce any sympathy you have toward this spirit.*

I prayed and asked the Holy Spirit to reveal any ways I might have been entangled by it. I admitted I was drawn to her strength but repulsed by her hatred. I renounced this attraction. Almost as an afterthought, I asked God, "Show me any ways I've adopted her practices."

Immediately, I remembered Jezebel's interaction with Ahab in 1 Kings 21. Ahab was depressed because his neighbor wouldn't sell him the family vineyard so Ahab could plant a vegetable garden close to his palace.

> But Naboth said to Ahab, "The LORD forbid that I should give you the inheritance of my fathers." (v. 3)

Ahab returned home sullen and so vexed he refused to eat.

And Jezebel his wife said to him, "Do you now govern Israel? Arise and eat bread and let your heart be cheerful; I will give you the vineyard of Naboth the Jezreelite." (v. 7)

Jezebel devised a plan to steal the land for her husband by misusing his authority.

So she wrote letters in Ahab's name and sealed them with his seal, and she sent the letters to the elders and the leaders who lived with Naboth in his city. And she wrote in the letters, "Proclaim a fast, and set Naboth at the head of the people. And set two worthless men opposite him, and let them bring a charge against him, saying, 'You have cursed God and the king.' Then take him out and stone him to death." (vv. 8–10)

The man was falsely accused, unjustly murdered, and Ahab took possession of the land for his vegetables.

At first, I saw no connection between myself and this queen who stole, lied, and murdered an innocent man over a garden. I wasn't after my neighbor's vineyard . . . but there was a letter. One I'd written on John's behalf. I wanted to expose the toxic work environment. It was time the lying, backbiting, threats, and manipulation stopped. The senior pastor needed to know what was going on and address it. If John wasn't willing to do this, I would for our family's sake. (Which, in hindsight, would have gotten John fired for sure!)

I heard the Holy Spirit admonish me: *I am doing a deep work in your husband, and your desire to protect him will prevent it. Throw away the letter and trust Me.*

I thought I was helping. But when I got gut-level honest, what I wanted was to control the outcome. Yikes! I shared all of this with John. We agreed God would be our defense and surrendered the entire situation to the care of our heavenly Father. This battle was far too big for us to handle in any other way but with prayer. It wasn't long until everything came to light while John was out of the country on a mission trip. God rescued us without any help from me. The lessons we learned out of the whole mess became John's book *The Bait of Satan*, which has touched the lives of untold millions in over 120 languages. But I almost got in the way of all of that.

The reason I share this encounter is twofold. First, there is a very strong pull on us women to take matters into our own hands on our own terms. The spirit of this age and the brokenness of our past encourage us toward control rather than surrender. Please know I am not suggesting anyone should be silent when abuse is present that puts others in peril. Our reputation was under attack, but we were never unsafe. I wanted to step in on behalf of our family, but God had a larger rescue in mind.

And now we are in a battle for the very identity of womanhood, the safety of our children, and the health of our families, and this one can't be waged in our strength alone. This will require engaging heaven. This fight for female is too big for us.

> Now all glory to God, who is able, through his mighty power at work within us, to accomplish infinitely more than we might ask or think. (Eph. 3:20 NLT)

Second, God is the One who is able. He is able when we are incapable. He steps in when we realize we are in over our heads and we surrender. I was offended. John was offended. We were wounded and mistreated. But God had a redemptive purpose in it all. He not only rescued us, He redeemed the entire mess, and what we learned in the process has been a source of rescue for others. Currently there is an epidemic of offense within and outside the body of Christ. The message about freedom from the trap of offense in *The Bait of Satan* is more relevant now than ever.

No matter who we are, submission to God is our first step before engaging in spiritual battles. David modeled this dynamic repeatedly. Even though he was a seasoned leader and skillful warrior, he sought God's counsel first.

> And David inquired of the LORD, "Shall I pursue after this band? Shall I overtake them?" He answered him, "Pursue, for you shall surely overtake and shall surely rescue." (1 Sam. 30:8)

If we believe God is our source of strategy and strength, why wouldn't we go to Him first for guidance? Proverbs 3:5–6 says,

> Trust in the LORD with all your heart,
>   and do not lean on your own understanding.
> In all your ways acknowledge him,
>   and he will make straight your paths.

You can trust God with your entire heart. My understanding has failed me more times than I can count. He wants to be involved in all our ways. There is nothing beneath His notice and there is nothing too heavy for Him to lift. In these days of twists and turns, we need the only One who can see around the corners to give us a straight path forward. This is echoed in James 4:6–7, which tells us,

> "God opposes the proud but gives grace to the humble." Submit yourselves therefore to God. Resist the devil, and he will flee from you.

For the rest of this chapter, I'll discuss the strategies for spiritual warfare that I see in Scripture.

Make Sure You Are In the Know

Before even thinking about engaging in any type of spiritual warfare, be sure you're in the know. Knowing about something is not the same as knowing it, any more than knowing about someone is the same as knowing them. We see this play out in Acts 19:

> Then some of the itinerant Jewish exorcists undertook to invoke the name of the Lord Jesus over those who had evil spirits, saying, "I adjure you by the Jesus whom Paul proclaims." Seven sons of a Jewish high priest named Sceva were doing this. But the evil spirit answered them, "Jesus I know, and Paul I recognize, but who are you?" And the man in whom was the evil spirit leaped on them, mastered all of them and overpowered them, so that they fled out of that house naked and wounded. (vv. 13–16)

We need daughters who have an intimate rather than itinerant knowledge of Jesus. One evil spirit dominated seven grown men because they knew about the authority in the name of Jesus but didn't have any themselves. Demons know who the children of God are. When you believed, you were marked by the Spirit of the Most High. Only those who are in Christ have authority in His name.

Check and Protect Your Heart

Pride has the power to blindside all of us. Warfare in the Spirit requires God's grace and guidance. Though it may sound counterintuitive, our spiritual battles begin with surrender and should always be motivated by love because love always includes a "for." For example, I hate adultery because I am *for* the covenant of marriage; therefore, I fight to help others build strong marriages.

I constantly ask myself, *Is this a fight for or just against?* If my answer is *against*, then I need to step back and check my motives. The answer to that question is my why. If our motive is wrong, the outcome will be compromised as well.

Another question to ask yourself and answer: *Is this within my circle of control or influence?* If it is, seek God for the correct approach. Move forward in the right frame of mind. Human anger is a great motivator and an awful ruler. Let your emotions and feelings act like army scouts. They are resourceful at locating the enemy, but the Holy Spirit draws up the battle plan.

> Know this, my beloved brothers: let every person be quick to hear, slow to speak, slow to anger; for **the anger of man does not produce the righteousness of God.** (James 1:19–20, emphasis added)

Anger uses up a lot of energy without moving people toward being rightly related to God or one another. As someone who is half-Sicilian, I understand being slow to anger is far easier said than done, but the fact that we've neglected doing anger well is what has fostered a lot of the current disconnect and chaos we are experiencing. James 1:20 in The Message reads, "God's righteousness doesn't grow from human anger."

What are we growing with our angry words and actions? All I see is a harvest of increased anxiety and anger. Women are angry at men. Women are angry with each other. I wrote the letter because I didn't like my husband being attacked, but I tossed the letter because we were in a conflict with something far bigger than my anger could have navigated.

The devil loves to encourage us to vent our anger in the wrong places. We all have the right to be angry but not to be destructive. You have every right to be upset but not to sin. Share your frustration with people who can move you toward a solution. If you don't have someone in your life who holds that place, then take it to the One who is the answer. When we submit to God, we come under His protection and authority.

Listening to the news and the insanity of our day can be overwhelming. Add in the division and sin within the church and

I want to scream. There are times when I want to pick up my phone and let everyone have it. But if I take it out on people, I become part of the problem rather than the solution. Rather than call people out, we should call one another up to a higher standard. God loves people; people are not the problem. Satan is. Put down your phone and be slow to speak until your anger is resolved.

> God loves people; people are not the problem.

There are so many battles I have had to fight more than once because I missed this lesson the first few times around.

We also need to make sure we check our posture. Demons love it when our hearts are divided because they know we do not have the authority to confront what we agree with. The moment I renounced any sympathy I had toward the Jezebel spirit, any entanglement I may have had with it was broken and I gained a sensitivity that helped me avoid any future alignments. Obedience to God creates divine alignment, the highest form of spiritual warfare.

Know What You're Wrestling

Who are you wrestling with? For example, you may feel like you are in a fight with your husband. You think he is insensitive, but what is really going on is that the enemy is trying to destroy your marriage. When an argument or disagreement of any kind gets overly charged, there is usually something more behind it. I remember John once called me from Southeast Asia and was super tense. He was exhausted and unreasonable. He went off on a rant. I don't even remember what the rant was about; I just knew he was in a highly charged, oppressive environment. I let him know we could talk about it again when he was stateside. When he got home, he apologized for mishandling the conversation. I assured him there was no need because I understood he was in a demonic atmosphere that had magnified everything.

And other times we're just experiencing people in need.

Recently, on an airport Skylink train, a woman started cussing violently. Everyone looked at her, then turned away, but I sensed she was troubled and approached her.

"Are you okay?" I asked.

She peppered her response with a collection of choice words. She was afraid she was about to miss her next flight. She'd been up for over thirty-four hours and, in a state of exhaustion, had gone to the wrong gate. I asked where she was going and discovered we were on the same flight. I assured her that we were going to make it. I am not sure she believed me. As we changed trains, she berated herself for being stupid. I asked her what type of work she did. She was a flight nurse.

"Then you are far from stupid," I said. "Listen, my husband's at the gate waiting for me. If you can run with me, we will make it!" We ran like our hair was on fire and made the flight.

It would have been easy to mistake her anger as combative, but the person she was the most frustrated with was herself. Sometimes it's not demonic; sometimes people are exhausted and simply need someone to run alongside them. If we truly believe we are ambassadors on a rescue mission for heaven, we need to stop fighting the ones we are assigned to help. People are rarely the problem, but at times you can be their answer.

Our true enemies are invisible and not of this world.

> For we do not wrestle against flesh and blood, but against the rulers, against the authorities, against the cosmic powers over this present darkness, against the spiritual forces of evil in the heavenly places. (Eph. 6:12)

Sit with this list from Ephesians a moment: rulers, authorities, cosmic powers over our present darkness. Spiritual forces of evil in the heavenly realms. Evil is becoming increasingly evident, but I doubt that any of us have ever met any of these forces. We meet the people they attack, use, and control. N. T. Wright translates the same verse this way:

> The warfare we're engaged in, you see, isn't against flesh and blood. It's against the leaders, against the authorities, against the powers that rule the world in this dark time, against the wicked spiritual elements in the heavenly places.[1]

If we are not fighting with flesh and blood, then people are not the problem. Spiritual forces cannot be humanly handled. It will require the leading of the Spirit. We have spiritual authority when we are under His authority. We do not have power in our name but in the supremacy of the name of Jesus.

Don't Be Careless with the Sacred

> Do not give dogs what is holy, and do not throw your pearls before pigs, lest they trample them underfoot and turn to attack you. (Matt. 7:6)

I love my dog, but she would have no idea how to handle anything holy. In the same way, pigs and pearls have no business in the muck together. When we are careless with any sacred entrustment, we open ourselves up to attack. Matthew 7:6 is a clear warning not to mix the holy with the profane. In life there are conversations and prayers that are holy in one setting that would be inappropriate in another. For example, sexual intimacy between a husband and wife is holy, but if you put it online it becomes pornographic. The right thing in the wrong setting becomes the wrong thing.

During the last presidential election, the church broadcast passionate prayers that did not seem to be answered and prophecies that didn't prove true. Both of these would have been better kept private. This caused widespread and unnecessary confusion. The Message puts the same verse this way:

Don't be flip with the sacred. Banter and silliness give no honor to God. Don't reduce holy mysteries to slogans. In trying to be relevant, you're only being cute and inviting sacrilege.

Let us be careful to measure our words and remember that not everything we say or do needs to be broadcast. Let's not dishonor God and the gift of prayer with foolish public misuse. The Lord's prayer invites God's kingdom and will into every situation without telling God what that will should be or how we think He should perform it. I do believe one way to avoid this type of irreverence is to know and pray the Word of God.

Pray the Word

There are times when our circumstances leave us gutted and without words. Perhaps it is an argument that remains unresolved or a long season of repeated disappointment and discouragement that feels as though it will never end. Scripture gives us the words when we don't know what to say or pray. When I feel over- or underwhelmed, the Psalms are where I find comfort. When I need wisdom, I turn to Proverbs. When I need a dose of prophetic awe, I go to the book of Isaiah. The Gospels are where I can meet Jesus and watch Him interact with others. God's Word touches us because it is alive. The Word of God resonates so deeply because it has the power to create.

> The LORD merely spoke,
>   and the heavens were created.
> He breathed the word,
>   and all the stars were born. (Ps. 33:6 NLT)

We've been granted the privilege of words. God's Word is an eternal, invincible, and invisible sword. When I wrote *Girls with Swords*, I was given different swords: a machete from Costa

Rica, a dagger from Jordan, and a women's sword from Pakistan. None of which I'd know how to use. But that is okay because our swords are spoken and alive. They know what to do even when we do not.

> For the word of God is living and active, sharper than any two-edged sword, piercing to the division of soul and of spirit, of joints and of marrow, and discerning the thoughts and intentions of the heart. (Heb. 4:12)

The medium of prayer connects us with an unseen realm that is far more real and permanent than the one we live in each day.

> We look not at the things which are seen, but at the things which are not seen: for the things which are seen are temporal; but the things which are not seen are eternal. (2 Cor. 4:18 KJV)

This is where our battles are won. We wrestle first in prayer. There are times when our prayers need a bit more from us. I once spoke to a large gathering of youth girls, and afterward one of them approached me. She took me aside and in whispered words told me she was struggling with an eating disorder. She knew I had experienced freedom from an eating disorder and asked me to pray for her. I took her in my arms and prayed everything I knew how to pray. But I didn't feel a release. I hugged her and turned to a group of girls who had been waiting to speak to me. But as she was exiting the room, I saw a shadowed form follow her. I recognized that dark spirit. I called out the girl's name. She turned my way.

"Don't listen to it!" I yelled.

She nodded, but I saw resignation on her countenance. She knew it was following her. She knew the wrestling match was going to continue. That night, her face and the shadow were all I could see. I didn't understand why I had not sensed a shift when

I prayed for her. I knew it was God's will to see her walk in freedom. I had experienced that very freedom myself decades earlier. I tossed and turned all night in my hotel room. Then around two a.m. I heard a passage of Scripture that gave me my answer.

However, this kind does not go out except by prayer and fasting. (Matt. 17:21 NKJV)

I had my answer. I would fast and then pray with her again. I had another session the next day with the youth girls. This time when I prayed with her, there was freedom. I knew it and she knew it. We kept in contact for several years after that, and she confirmed God's faithfulness. She married and had a beautiful family even though she'd been told that children might never be in her future. Tragically, this verse has disappeared from several of the current Bible translations. But I believe in the power of fasting.

When we pray and obey the Spirit of God, the authority of God's kingdom comes to bear upon our challenges. The Word and the Holy Spirit are our constant guides. I often think it would be nice if we could have a Zoom call or video chat with our heavenly Father. Then He could show us directly and precisely what to do. Instead, we walk it out by faith, which means we perceive His heart rather than hear direct quotes, with His Word shining a light on the path before us.

Deal with What You May Have Dabbled In

I adored my father and as a very young child I watched scary shows with him to prove how courageous I was. But whenever an alien or sea monster was a bit too frightening, I'd hide behind his back. As a teen I watched scary movies in theaters with friends and boyfriends. Even if I was terrified, I'd go back for more. One Christmas, I was given a Ouija board. It was an object we played with at slumber parties. I also had an astrology pillow for my friends to sign when they slept over. Occult practices were slipped into my childhood as though the paranormal was normal.

I knew darkness and evil were real, but it wasn't until I became a Christian that I discovered the power of light. Early on in my Christian walk, I renounced all agreements I'd unknowingly made with the occult through blatant rebellion, sexual promiscuity, astrology, ungodly vows, and several other things the Holy Spirit brought to my memory. I challenge you to do the same. There is something so beautiful about coming before the Lord and laying it all before Him. No matter what your past, no matter what your family's past, you can be the beginning of a thousand generations who love God and keep His commandments. At the close of this chapter, I've included a prayer framed with Scriptures for you to do this. I would encourage you to fast or take communion before or after working your way through this prayer.

Guard the Atmosphere of Your Home

This can be as simple as creating a different atmosphere by playing worship music. And it can be as difficult as resolving conflicts when there is still disagreement.

> Be angry and do not sin; do not let the sun go down on your anger, and give no opportunity to the devil. (Eph. 4:26–27)

Don't go to bed angry; it opens the door to the devil, and you don't want to invite him in. Not with your husband, not with your children, not with a friend, not with an enemy, not with an employer or employee, and not with strangers on social media whom you have no way of speaking to. If you can't come to a resolution before you go to bed, put it to rest and come up with a plan and a time to address it later. John and I set a time the very next day to discuss it. Be aware of what you allow into your home through your television. I'm shocked by how much demonic is slipped into the current programming. Monitor what your children can access online. This could be as simple as keeping the laptop in the kitchen.

Remember, Persecution Is Promised

> Dear friends, don't be surprised at the fiery trials you are going through, as if something strange were happening to you. (1 Pet. 4:12 NLT)

In many ways God used trials to build the early church. The dragon wasn't happy about an uncontained gospel of Jesus Christ. And yet Peter's words speak to us today. Be prepared for the fiery trials being a bit more intense than attacks on social media. Peter warned us that we're going to go through some stuff! You will be tested when you decide to fight for all that it means to be female: to be wise, kind, nurturing, godly, motherly, strategic, and protective. There will be resistance when you make bold declarations of repentance and alliance to Christ and turn from cultural definitions. Jesus warned His disciples in Matthew 10:16 about the environment they would be working in:

> Behold, I am sending you out as sheep in the midst of wolves, so be wise as serpents and innocent as doves.

Sheep are not the brightest animals. They need the protection of a shepherd. At first glance, this almost seems contradictory to the words of 1 Peter, which assure us we will have trials. How can we be sheep following a shepherd and yet still experience trials? Because our Shepherd never said we wouldn't go through trials; He just promised we wouldn't go through them alone.

Matthew 10:16 also encourages us to be wise or shrewd as serpents and innocent or as harmless as doves. Serpents are crafty and cunning. When you don't have arms and legs you need to make the best of your situation. Snakes choose their environment carefully because they lie in wait, hoping to ambush their unsuspecting victims.

A dove is a universal symbol of peace and reconciliation. Doves also symbolize forgiveness and release. If we merge these two—serpent and dove—we must be wise and aware that we are in a hostile territory, yet gentle and led by the Spirit.

———

Is there a situation you're trying to control that needs to be surrendered?

Is there a person you're trying to control but should turn over to God?

Ask the Holy Spirit if there is anything you've dabbled in or made unwitting agreements with that you feel you should renounce.

What is one thing you can do to fight in the Spirit instead of in your own strength?

Prayer for Renouncing Agreements with Evil

Dear heavenly Father,

I come before You in the name of Your precious Son, Jesus; I enter Your gates with thanksgiving and come into Your courts with praise. I am overwhelmed by Your gracious mercy and love for me, and I thank You for the mighty work of redemption You have wrought in my life.

Holy Spirit, I need You. Lead and guide me now. Jesus, You are my Lord. Heavenly Father, You are the God of heaven and earth, the great and awesome God, who keeps Your covenant of love with those who love You and obey Your commands. Let Your ear be attentive to hear the prayer of Your daughter.

I confess my sins and the sins of my father's house, every transgression we have committed against You. Forgive us for any and every way we have acted wickedly toward You. But You, Lord, our God, are merciful and forgiving and sent Your Son, even though we have rebelled. We ask You to circumcise our hearts and roll away the sin, shame, and reproach of our pasts.

I confess and renounce my sin and the sins of my forefathers, for any and all involvement in the occult, witchcraft, or divination. [Pause and stay sensitive to add anything the Holy Spirit brings to your attention to specifically renounce before continuing. This may include, but certainly is not limited to, astrology, séances, horror movies, tarot cards, games, books, etc.] I renounce my involvement in these things and break their curse off my life and off the generations that follow after me.

I confess and renounce my sin and/or the sins of my forefathers in the area of drug and alcohol abuse. Father, close any door this may have opened in the spirit realm to sin, bondage, or oppression. I renounce my involvement with _____ [specifically call the drugs out by name, if applicable], and I break the power of their curse off my life and off the lives of my children, their children, and their children's children.

Father, I confess and renounce my sin and the sins of my forefathers for any and all involvement in sexual sin and all impurity, perversion, incest, and promiscuity. [Be sensitive here to specifically name the sins you are renouncing. Speak them out before Him without shame. There is nothing hidden—He knows each of them already and longs to remove their weight of guilt and shame from you. Then, when you are ready, proceed.]

Father, take the sword of Your Spirit and sever every ungodly sexual soul tie between me and _____. [Listen to the Holy Spirit and speak each name out as you hear it. It is quite possible the names may even be of those with whom you did not have intercourse but those with whom you were sexually or emotionally involved in a way that should be reserved for your husband or Savior alone.]

After speaking each name out individually, pray this:

Father, restore any fragments of my soul from these men [or women] by Your Spirit so that I might be whole, holy, and set apart for Your pleasure.

Father, I renounce the hold of every perverted and promiscuous image that may have entered through written or other forms of pornography. Forgive me for allowing vile and perverted images before my eyes. I make a covenant according to Psalm 101:3, and I will guard the issues of my heart by way of the gateway of my eyes. I will not allow any vile thing before my eyes. I renounce every unclean spirit, and I command it and its influence to leave my life.

Father, wash me in the cleansing blood of Jesus, for it alone has the power to cleanse and atone. I consecrate myself now as Your temple. By the power of Your Holy Spirit, remove all defilement of the spirit, soul, and flesh from the temple of my body. Fill me to overflowing with the indwelling of Your Holy Spirit. Open my eyes to see, my ears to hear, and my heart to receive all that You have for me. I am Yours. Have Your way in my life. Amen.

CHAPTER 5

The Fight for Generations

For the Son of man is come to seek and to save that which was lost.

Luke 19:10 KJV

Our Savior longs to restore vision to a generation who has lost theirs. Without a vision and a clear way forward, we lose our way. The enemy wants our children blindfolded with scraps of lies to strip them of divine hope. With hope out of the way, discouragement dominates our thoughts and fear has free rein. There is something fear wants to stop in your life—don't let it. Proverbs 29:18 tells us, "Where there is no prophetic vision the people cast off restraint."

Thankfully, God has a prophetic vision for the generations:

> In the last days it shall be, God declares,
> that I will pour out my Spirit on all flesh,

> and your sons and your daughters shall prophesy,
> and your young men shall see visions,
> and your old men shall dream dreams;
> even on my male servants and female servants
> in those days I will pour out my Spirit, and they shall
>   prophesy. (Acts 2:17–18)

Which raises the question, are we in the last days? Acts 2:17 opens with "in the last days," plural. As we study Scripture, we quickly discover God measures His days quite differently than we do. Second Peter 3:8 tells us,

> But do not overlook this one fact, beloved, that with the Lord one day is as a thousand years, and a thousand years as one day.

This could stretch the "last days" timeline to two thousand years. Either way it's time we say what God sees. God sees His Spirit poured out on our sons and daughters as well as on the old and the young. Our Father sees a generation prophesying repentance and a coming kingdom. God sees a renewing of dreams and visions for His servants. And yet, rather than echo God's Word, we've allowed harsh words to be spoken over the generations.

It's time we say what God sees.

We must be careful not to assume that where we are now is where we will always be. I believe we stand on the threshold of the way things are and the way God wants them to be. Things shift when God's Word is declared over the generations. Second Timothy 4:2–3 admonishes us on the importance of the Word:

> Preach the word; be ready in season and out of season; reprove, rebuke, and exhort, with complete patience and teaching. For the time is coming when people will not endure sound teaching, but having itching ears they will accumulate for themselves teachers to suit their own passions.

God's Word is alive and constructive. It has the power to counter every destructive word spoken by the enemy or even by other well-meaning Christians. God's transformative Word can renew minds and redeem what's been lost by making all things new. You don't need to take counsel with strangers online; the Holy Spirit has promised to be your Counselor. Therapy has the power to break patterns, and the Holy Spirit has the power of transformation.

Open your Bible and ask the Holy Spirit to speak to you. Then don't be surprised if God speaks to you as you read the passages. Pause and listen for the still, small voice that whispers wisdom and insight that you could never think of on your own. The words of the prophet Isaiah still stand as an invitation to all of us.

> Come now, let us reason together, says the LORD:
> though your sins are like scarlet,
>   they shall be as white as snow;
> though they are red like crimson,
>   they shall become like wool. (1:18)

And what does He ask of us in return? That we be willing and obedient (v. 19). He didn't ask for perfection; we've proved that's not possible. He asked that we'd be willing and obedient rather than willful and disobedient. This is a reasonable request and a conversation He invites all of us to have. The Lord exchanges our sin and iniquity for His righteousness. There is no need to make excuses or lay blame. Own it for what it is—sin—and surrender it to the only One who turns screaming scarlet radiant white. Jesus longs to heal what life has torn, fix what life has broken, and wash what life has dirtied.

People will disappoint you, not because they want to but because they are human. God will not. Don't confuse people with God or you will end up looking in the wrong places for what only God gives. The pursuit of more things, other places or pathways, other genders, another husband, another wife, another boyfriend, or another girlfriend will not satisfy your longing. He is your Source.

A Generation of Warriors

If others call you a victim, don't believe them. It's the enemy's tactic to keep you contained or weak. You don't need excuses. You're not a victim; you are a threat. It is one of the many reasons why the enemy has worked overtime to confuse a generation of warriors with half-truths. It is obvious there is something in and on you that the enemy desperately wants to abort. It is why the dragon plagues this generation with unholy, violent, and hopeless imagery. He wants you driven by fear, anger, and lust. He knows God has called you to something more. God wants you set apart for Him.

> You're not a victim; you are a threat.

Don't give any more time to your detractors. It's time to get serious and remember—there are far more cheering you on than those who mock and jeer. Hebrews 12:1 tells us,

> Therefore, since we are surrounded by so great a cloud of witnesses, let us also lay aside every weight, and sin which clings so closely, and let us run with endurance the race that is set before us.

You were made for this race at this time. But you will not be able to run it if you are carrying burdens and sin. Don't be afraid; it is time to leave behind the patterns of sin and trauma. They will only hinder you from moving forward and rob you of the life you long for. Be willing to take some steps forward, and as you do God will reveal the path before you. God wants to speak to and through you. In addition to God healing you, He wants to heal through you. God wants you free to see others freed by your testimony. Any areas of our lives that matter to us matter to Him. Hurt by a friend? Bring it to Him. Ridiculed for your beliefs? Bring it to Him. Doubting your purpose? Bring it to Him.

You reconnect with your Creator by developing a sensitivity to His voice. More likely than not, this will mean shutting down your computer and turning off your phone. Interruptions and distractions pull you away from the divine attraction. Distractions keep you from gaining traction and moving forward in freedom. When you travel the roads of the internet for too long, you risk forgetting what the path under your feet feels like. The importance of pulling away to find time with your Creator cannot be overemphasized. We discover who we are in the presence of God rather than in the presence of people. It is in the pursuit of the divine that we discover our wholeness. As you pursue knowing Him, He reveals *you*.

The younger generation is fighting a battle within themselves that culture is trying to fix from the outside. They have a divine discontentment that religion does not satisfy. The answer they seek is not found by transitioning or even de-transitioning. Their answer runs deeper than the surgeon's knife could reach or a pharmaceutical could create. This generation will not rest until they experience transformation, and Jesus is our only way to transformation.

In every way He is able to sympathize with our weakness and struggles.

Jesus also understands the pain of racism, prejudice, and persecution. He suffered as a victim of all three. He grew up under the oppression of the Roman Empire and yet was able to establish a kingdom that will have no end. As a Jewish descendant of the tribe of Judah, He would have seen the beginnings of the horrors of anti-Semitism.

To this day we see evidence of this hatred. Jews have been consistently persecuted, stripped of their land, and enslaved. First Egypt, then Babylon, Rome, and the Crusades. They were dispersed again and faced persecution, loss, and death under

Hitler and Stalin. Their ashes are scattered throughout much of Eastern Europe, and tragically they have been attacked in their homeland of Israel and even in the United States.

Isaiah 53:3 tells us this about Jesus:

> He was despised and rejected by men,
>   a man of sorrows and acquainted with grief;
> and as one from whom men hide their faces
>   he was despised, and we esteemed him not.

Jesus was rejected by the very ones He came to save.

> He came to his own, and his own people did not receive him. (John 1:11)

He understands the pain of rejection more than I ever will. As I've written this book, I've wrestled. What do I hope my words will accomplish? The words that spring into my mind are restoration, redemption, revelation, and rescue. I want women to remember who they are and recover a mother's heart and mindset. This generation is poised for revival. Yet if the dragon has his way, he will put an end to their legacy.

According to recent data, by the close of this century 183 countries are projected not to have enough births to maintain their current population. That's over 90 percent of the nations.[1] Research projects that millennials and Gen Z will not have enough children to sustain the American population.[2]

Depopulation is a threat, not an answer. The enemy of our souls knows that the devaluing of children and the destruction of the family dismantle culture and corrupt the government and educational systems.

Yet, in the middle of this mess, God is redeeming and activating a generation. God loves the LGBTQ+ community. There is nothing they can do or become that will move them outside of

His love and reach. Let's make sure we are not blocking their entrance.

God wants to reach and restore. It is His love rather than religion that brings the rejected and violated into holiness and wholeness. He loves the daughters who were lied to, stripped of their female form, and handed back a false identity. He calls them by name. We've all looked for the right thing from wrong people, ideologies, and places. Churches and ministers have disappointed us. Scripture has been twisted or misused both to condone and to condemn. People

> It is His love rather than religion that brings the rejected and violated into holiness and wholeness.

have been abused by the very ones charged with their protection. In our search for the truth, the enemy has told us lies. But never Jesus and never our Father. Luke 14 shows us how God fills His house.

> But he said to him, "A man once gave a great banquet and invited many. And at the time for the banquet he sent his servant to say to those who had been invited, 'Come, for everything is now ready.' But they all alike began to make excuses. The first said to him, 'I have bought a field, and I must go out and see it. Please have me excused.' And another said, 'I have bought five yoke of oxen, and I go to examine them. Please have me excused.' And another said, 'I have married a wife, and therefore I cannot come.' So the servant came and reported these things to his master. Then the master of the house became angry and said to his servant, 'Go out quickly to the streets and lanes of the city, and bring in the poor and crippled and blind and lame.' And the servant said, 'Sir, what you commanded has been done, and still there is room.' And the master said to the servant, 'Go out to the highways and hedges and compel people to come in, that my house may be filled. For I tell you, none of those men who were invited shall taste my banquet.'" (vv. 16–24)

God has beloved children waiting to be found. Many now live on the highways (internet), desperately searching, and among the hedges of life (those labeled outsiders), and God is asking us to go out where they are and compel them to come to His house for a banquet.

Just as we were loved before we drew our first breath, they were loved. Loved as the enemy distorted God's handiwork in an attempt to steal or sexualize their identity. Loved as they struggled to find community, love, and acceptance online or at school. Loved when they tried to find healing in the arms of yet another man, or yet another woman. Loved as they tried on the identity of a man. Like all of us, they are loved but lost until they discover His love. Then this generation will be empowered to walk in their identity as children of the Most High God.

Now the Lord of the harvest is asking us to love in the same way. And we better figure out this love quickly because there is a sense of urgency. Let us not forget that "we love because he first loved us" (1 John 4:19).

Don't let this idea of loving intimidate you.

You don't have to win arguments to love people.

You don't have to agree with people to love them.

You don't have to look like them to love them.

People do not need to change for you to love them; His love changes everything.

God loved us in our sin.

Love is not an endorsement of sin; love is the escape from sin.

When we love God, we hate what He hates and love what He loves. What God loves is people. God loves the lost. God hates the death and destruction of His children. God *is* love.

Arguments will fail but love never will.

Social programs will fail but love never fails.

Politicians will fail but not love.

People may fail you but love never fails.

I fear we've become so divided in our opinions and pursuits that we've forgotten what really matters. We keep inviting the healthy or the busy to the table when God is asking us to reach the broken. Are we wasting time arguing with those who already feel they have all the answers and neglecting conversations with those who want to know the One who is the answer? Combative disagreements on social media do not draw others to Christ any more than compromising the message of the cross will set the captives free.

> We keep inviting the healthy or the busy to the table when God is asking us to reach the broken.

Oh, that we might learn this, that I might learn this. Jesus needs us to leave behind our busy religions and look for those who see themselves as outsiders. This happens when we share how He took the unbearable weight of our sin and shame upon Himself. Stop pretending and start testifying about His saving grace; that is the way we lift the name of Jesus. The One who rescued us will rescue them. Can we believe Jesus wants to reveal Himself to the broken and angry?

Recently, revivals have broken out on a number of college campuses. One began as students confessed their sins, worshiped, and testified. I was thrilled to see an outpouring of God's Spirit on our campuses. But almost immediately, critics questioned the revival's theology. I would argue that something can be pure and orchestrated by God's Spirit even if it is not perfect. Be careful with criticism. It is dangerous to attack the imperfect yet pure. At this point I am weary of the perfect in form but impure in motive. For every daughter who is weary of looking at *the place and pattern* of worship and is ready to embrace the *presence and spirit,* Jesus understands.

But the time is coming—it has, in fact, come—when what you're called will not matter and where you go to worship will not matter.

It's who you are and the way you live that count before God. Your worship must engage your spirit in the pursuit of truth. That's the kind of people the Father is out looking for: those who are simply and honestly *themselves* before him in their worship. (John 4:23 MSG, italics in the original)

Worship should be led by the Spirit and focused on the One who is truth. Only He satisfies the thirsty, lonely daughters who are tired of drawing dead water from the muddy wells of legalism or from wells tainted with sin and shame. Beautiful daughters, dare to dream and leave behind your regret, disappointment, and remorse. Anger and vengeance will never quench our thirst; these emotions only leave us disillusioned, frustrated, and desperate for something more. When a generation wanders the desert of disappointment and deconstruction, religion will not satisfy their souls. But in the wilds they discover the Rock that gives water.

Jesus was the Temple that was destroyed and rebuilt, referenced in Mark 14:58: "We heard him say, 'I will destroy this Temple made with human hands, and in three days I will build another, made without human hands'" (NLT).

This generation seeks temples built with hearts, not hands. They will not be content with religious forms void of the Spirit. His body was broken that we might be one body with Him. Jesus paid the ultimate price to redeem us, but at times I fear we have forgotten all that His death purchased.

Or do you not know that your body is a temple of the Holy Spirit within you, whom you have from God? **You are not your own,** for you were bought with a price. **So glorify God in your body.** (1 Cor. 6:19–20, emphasis added)

If we were purchased, our lives are not our own. Too little is said about honoring God with our bodies. One way our female bodies glorify God is our capacity to carry life. Women are uniquely crafted as warriors for life. Motherhood, whether by birth or adoption, is warfare. Others advocate for life in other ways. Please read the words of Mother Teresa before the Supreme Court of the United States in 1994:

> America needs no words from me to see how your decision in Roe vs. Wade has deformed a great nation. The so-called right to abortion has pitted mothers against their children and women against men. It has sown violence and discord at the heart of the most intimate human relationships. It has aggravated the derogation of the father's role in an increasingly fatherless society. It has portrayed the greatest of gifts—a child—as a competitor, an intrusion and an inconvenience. It has nominally accorded mothers unfettered dominion over the dependent lives of their physically dependent sons and daughters. And, in granting this unconscionable power, it has exposed many women to unjust and selfish demands from their husbands or other sexual partners.[3]

There is mercy for our past, but there must be a way forward or we will lose future generations. Let's honor God with our bodies and value children the way God values them. Children are a gift that abortion destroys. When children are not wanted, protected, or provided for, humanity turns to self-fulfillment instead of supporting generational legacies.

What God makes is not ours to unmake. Marriage is the precursor of family. Marriage is a flawed institution because it involves two flawed people. Yet it is still the healthiest and most productive unit for raising children. God can, does, and will bless single parents who navigate raising children on their own. He is and will always be a Father to the fatherless. But the best hope is healthy families who work together to build legacies that honor God.

Listen to how God describes what happens when a man and woman are joined together in marriage:

> Did he not make them one, with a portion of the Spirit in their union? And what was the one God seeking? Godly offspring. So guard yourselves in your spirit, and let none of you be faithless to the wife of your youth. (Mal. 2:15)

Marriage is a sacrament that involves the Spirit of God. Through this sacrament He weaves the two into one. The current cultural attack against marriage is spiritual as well as physical. The Message frames the purpose and involvement of God in marriage this way:

> GOD, not you, made marriage. His Spirit inhabits even the smallest details of marriage. And what does he want from marriage? Children of God, that's what. So guard the spirit of marriage within you. Don't cheat on your spouse. (Mal. 2:15)

Our Father God is multigenerational as the God of Abraham, Isaac, and Jacob. Think of it, the hope of Abraham's grandson Jacob was in his loins even as he waited in faith for his son Isaac. God chose Abram (whose name was later enlarged to Abraham) as our father of faith when he had yet to have the son of promise.

> For I have chosen him, that he may command his children and his household after him to keep the way of the LORD by doing righteousness and justice, so that the LORD may bring to Abraham what he has promised him. (Gen. 18:19)

I've included The Message translation of this verse as well because it lends more clarity:

> Yes, I've settled on him as the one to train his children and future family to observe GOD's way of life, live kindly and generously

and fairly, so that GOD can complete in Abraham what he promised him.

Gendercide was used when God's people awaited first their deliverance and then their king. When God chose Israel as His people, it wasn't long before the enemy moved against them. First, it was Pharaoh who ordered the murder of the Hebrew male babies during Egyptian oppression. Yet Moses escaped. Baby boys were the target again under Roman rule as well; King Herod ordered the murder of all boys two and under born within the region of Bethlehem. Scripture describes the agony of their mothers.

> A voice was heard in Ramah,
>   weeping and loud lamentation,
> Rachel weeping for her children;
>   she refused to be comforted, because they are no more.
>   (Matt. 2:18)

In the past century, we've witnessed the atrocities of the Holocaust, two world wars, 73 million innocent lives ended by abortion globally *each year*,[4] and a century punctuated by genocides. Now we see gendercide again, but this time it is baby girls who are targeted. The decrease in the female population is estimated at 200 million due largely to male-based sex selection.[5] When we see this type of targeted attack against women, we must wonder why.

What Our Enemy Knows

What I said in chapter 1 bears repeating: I believe the enemy's focus has shifted to women because Jesus is coming back for His bride, the church. Satan wants women eliminated and every concept of marriage undermined. He has successfully distorted

THE FIGHT FOR FEMALE

the concept of a pure bride who watches or waits for her bride-groom. He wants us to think of marriage as a hindrance rather than a catalyst for growth. Marriage fosters responsibility and unconditional love and confronts areas of selfishness in a way no other relationship can. Tragically, declining marriage rates translate to increased cultural immaturity and declining birth rates.

According to a recent Pew Research Center report, a quarter of millennials will reach the age of forty without marrying.[6] There are several reasons for this trend: student loan debt, financial independence, prioritization of careers, a lack of affordable housing, fear of divorce, and less interest in marriage and childbearing. Another reason is that sex is readily available outside of marriage. Rather than commit to the work of building an intimate life and family with one person, a vast number choose to remain single and have sex with many.

During my lifetime, sexual intimacy has taken a downward spiral. The sexual revolution of the 1960s and '70s was pushed forward by "an unlikely coalition of scientists, feminists, hippies, and gay rights activists who believed that a freer, more progressive sexuality was in order."[7] They united to facilitate access to contraception and abortions. These innovations increased the ease of sexual relations outside of marriage and led to a rise in divorces. Increased promiscuity led to a sharp uptick in STDs (or STIs).[8] In the 1980s, HIV/AIDS entered the scene, and for a brief period, panic checked the number of sexual partners and practices people were willing to engage in. After a while, this fear abated even though HIV/AIDS-related illnesses still claim around 600,000 lives per year, and an estimated 39 million live with HIV.[9] Homosexual and bisexual relations were mainstreamed, then sanctioned with the legalization of same-sex marriage in the US in 2015. When pornography went from print only to online, access and addiction increased exponentially. Porn addiction affects millions globally. Men are 543 percent more likely than women to look at porn, and nearly 200,000 people in the US are considered porn addicts. In the US, 40 million adults regularly visit porn sites, and 35 percent of all internet downloads are porn related.[10] Pedophiles are in the process of being renamed MAP (minor-attracted people),[11] and a Princeton professor of bioethics endorsed a study normalizing bestiality, renamed zoophilia (human sex with animals).[12]

The sexualization of our youth has evolved at an alarming speed. We have an epidemic of sex and a famine of intimacy. "Making love," long considered a sacred act with the power to create life and unite two in a marriage covenant, changed when it became "sex," then sex was reduced to an individual's right to gratification rather than mutual pleasure and intimacy.

Our moral freefall has exceeded the dire predictions of Aldous Huxley's *Brave New World*, a place without monogamy, bodily autonomy, or family. A world where children are created in labs (an advance estimated to be five years away[13]) and everyone takes soma, an anti-anxiety med, to ward off questions. The cultural mantra of Huxley's brave new world is "Every one belongs to every one else."[14] In our day, the mantra is rapidly becoming "Everyone can do anything to everyone or everything," with the involvement of people optional. To undermine and destroy the next generation, the dragon who once whispered now shouts . . .

Alone is better.

Abortion is healthcare.

Your body, your choice.

Women don't need men.

Marriage ends in divorce.

Pursue a career; delay a family.

Children are inconveniences that ruin your body.

Uncomfortable? Your assigned body is wrong—change it.

Parents can't be trusted. Don't talk to them; trust the experts.

We can no longer be passive; it is time to be proactive. Live your life in such a way that others see what you believe. Be kind. Be truthful. Call people up rather than out. Speak up for those who have been silenced. Invite a younger couple over for dinner and invest in the generations behind you. Open up conversations with those you'd normally consider outsiders. You'll be shocked how much you can learn and how many stereotypes will be confronted simply by sitting across the table from others.

Fighting for Female in Your Home

If you are married, love your husband. Work out your problems, with God in the center. Honor one another in front of your children. Gather the tools that you need to build a marriage that will give your children hope for a marriage in their future. Rather than complain about your marriage, celebrate it. Marriages are hard, but growing together is worthwhile.

If you have children, don't act like they are a bother when they are a reward. Psalm 127:3–5 tells us,

> Children are a heritage from the LORD,
>   the fruit of the womb a reward.
> Like arrows in the hand of a warrior
>   are the children of one's youth.
> Blessed is the man
>   who fills his quiver with them!
> He shall not be put to shame
>   when he speaks with his enemies in the gate.

Children are a blessing, not a burden. They are our ultimate wealth. We live on through our children. They reach places we can never touch and see what we can only glimpse now. Our children are arrows shot into our future. They will live in the victory of the battles we've fought and fight battles that are not yet before us. The psalmist refers to children as arrows in the hand of a warrior, proving the point that the enemy knows the next generation is a threat (Ps. 127:4–5). Aim them well.

Enjoy your family. Share meals and conversation. Play with your children. Be careful whose homes you allow them to spend the night in. Go on walks and talk about everything. Ask questions and listen, really listen. Keep them offline and engaged with your family life. Help them choose godly friends. Make your home a sanctuary of laughter, learning, and love. Include like-minded families in your friendship circle.

If you are single or don't have children, look for those who need a godmother, mentor, or friend. Do things you love. Adopt a family.

What is the one thing you can do to honor God's design for generations?

What is one thing you can pray for to restore God's design for generations?

CHAPTER 6

The Fight for Lost and Found

*Whoever is careless with the truth in small matters cannot be
trusted with important matters.*

Albert Einstein

My carelessness has proved costly.

I returned home from my sophomore year at university and discovered my gold chain necklace was missing. This was an accessory crisis for a teen of the '70s! Yet I distinctly remembered leaving the necklace in my bathroom drawer. I pulled every item out of the first drawer, then frantically rifled through all the drawers on my side of the cabinet. Then I pulled the drawers themselves out in case my necklace had fallen into the cabinet base but to no avail. I rifled through my bedroom drawers.

Nothing.

Had my necklace been stolen? Panicked at the thought of this loss, I yelled for my mother. "Mom, I can't find the gold chain Grandmother gave me!"

My mother appeared at the bathroom doorway. "I have it," she calmly volunteered.

I breathed a sigh of relief, glad to know its whereabouts. But when I asked for the necklace, I learned that it was lost to me even though it had been found. My mother let me know she'd be keeping the necklace . . . permanently. She made the argument that if I had valued the gift, I wouldn't have left it in a messy bathroom drawer. She showed me that an entire section of the necklace was bent out of shape. I had errantly forced the drawer closed with the chain in the gap.

I was furious.

I argued that the necklace wasn't hers to take. It was my grand-mother's gift to me! My mother reminded me that when I had been given the necklace, she'd raised the concern that I was too young to care for and appreciate its value. Sadly, my actions proved her assessment correct. I protested her decision several times and accused her of looking for a reason to take it from me, but my mother refused to relent. I never saw the necklace again.

More than four decades have passed, but I remember that lesson whenever I see a necklace that reminds me of the one I lost. You might think I remember because losing a gift from my grandmother was traumatic. But that is not why. It punctuated the fact that negligence has consequences. My mother's decision trained me how to handle items of value in the future. Careless-ness exacts a cost.

I only understood the necklace's value *after* it was lost. I had a jewelry box I could have put it in, but I'd tossed the necklace into a bathroom drawer because it was easier. Because I put it where it didn't belong, my necklace was damaged. The twisted links affected how the entire necklace laid.

Carelessness has cost me some plants. Carelessness has cost some relationships. Is it possible we've been careless with the gift of female? Did we allow our womanhood to be tossed in with things that didn't belong together? Is this why our connection with men has been bent out of shape?

Our Origin Story

We've been encouraged to be at odds with each other for so long, it's hard to remember a time when male and female were as beautifully connected as the links of a necklace. Let's return to our origin.

> Then the LORD God said, "It is not good that the man should be alone; I will make him a helper fit for him." (Gen. 2:18)

This is the first time Scripture references anything as "not good." It is important to note that God did not say that the man was not good; the man had purpose, he was active, and yet there was no intimate other. He was alone and that was not good. This is also the first time we see any lack highlighted amid the abundance of Eden. Paradise had a problem: its guardian was lonely.

> But for Adam there was not found a helper fit for him. (v. 20)

Every creature had a counterpart, a reflection, one that was alike yet uniquely different, except man. Man was created in the image of God but had none who reflected him. He longed for another, a union that was more than he knew how to describe or create.

His longing for something *more* worked a willingness to give more than we thought possible. It is the reason women continue to birth children, knowing both the risk and pain involved. It is the reason why service men and women leave all they love to fight wars to protect a future they may not be part of. I believe it's why God had the man lay down his life to bring forth the woman.

> So the LORD God caused a deep sleep to fall upon the man, and while he slept took one of his ribs and closed up its place with flesh. (v. 21)

There is no escaping the parallel between this and a surgery. God fashioned the woman from the man. God spoke everything in creation into being, but the man and woman were formed by His hands. The man yielded himself to God for the hope of what could be (the woman).

Woman was God's answer to the man's problem. The man needed the woman. What does this mean for us? It means our purpose, or creation origin, was an answer to the deep and painful problem of loneliness. Female is the intimate answer to male. They were fit for each other.

God did not create the woman to be dominated or abused by the man any more than He created the woman to manipulate or dominate the man. Woman was created to help him in a way only she could. I believe she was meant to be the guardian of his heart. I do think it is important to note that lending help does not make you less than . . . it makes you necessary. In her the man found what he lacked when he was alone. Her introduction changed what was "not good" to "very good."

The deep longing within him was alive and upright before him. His search was over. There was someone to share his flourishing Eden with (see v. 15).

Lending help does not make you less than . . . it makes you necessary.

Deep longings work their way into our dreams. I like to imagine that as the man slept, he dreamt of woman. She was his hope. This foreshadowed how Christ would lay down His life for the church, His bride. We are the bride born from His death. Jesus tells us in John 12:24, "Truly, truly, I say to you, unless a grain of wheat falls into the earth and dies, it remains alone; but if it dies, it bears much fruit."

The man knew what it meant to plant. The woman was the fruit born of the man's rib. Rabbinical and biblical texts refer to the creation of woman as her being formed by God from the man's rib. A few versions say the woman was taken from the man's side. Either phrasing tells us that out of the man came the woman. Before the fall, even their names reflected their divine alignment.

The Hebrew word for man is *ish* and the word for woman is *isha* or *ishah*. The genetic structure of man is the XY chromosome pair, and the structure of the woman is XX. It would seem our Creator isolated the man's X chromosome and raised it to the second power.

> The woman is part of the man; for this reason a man leaves his parents' house in order to find a woman who will restore him, as it were, to his original wholeness.
>
> Rav Chaim Navon[1]

At the dawn of creation, the woman knew she was from the man and for the man. She was always intended for him because she was designed for him and from him. But don't mistake the word *for* as a description of use or ownership.

> And God blessed them. And God said to them, "Be fruitful and multiply and fill the earth and subdue it, and have dominion over the fish of the sea and over the birds of the heavens and over every living thing that moves on the earth." (Gen. 1:28)

God gave the man and woman dominion over everything but each other. There was no power struggle; they were two, intimately united in body and purpose, and the enemy hated it. That's when things fell apart.

The Fall

> Now the serpent was more crafty than any other beast of the field that the LORD God had made.
>
> He said to the woman, "**Did God actually say,** 'You shall not eat of any tree in the garden'?" And the woman said to the serpent, "We may eat of the fruit of the trees in the garden, but God said, 'You shall not eat of the fruit of the tree that is in the midst of the garden, neither shall you touch it, lest you die.'" But the serpent said to the woman, "You will not surely die. For God knows that when you eat of it your eyes will be opened, and you will be like God, knowing good and evil." (Gen. 3:1–5, emphasis added)

The knowledge of good and evil is never a good substitute for the knowledge of God. Up until this point, the man and woman had walked in intimate fellowship with their Creator and with one another.

The serpent made her think she was missing something. I find it amazing that the woman grasped for something she was not to have (equality with God) and in the process lost something she already had the potential to possess (wisdom). By twisting God's words, the serpent appealed to their desire to be like God apart from Him. Then both the man and the woman grasped at a role that was not theirs to take. Ages later, the woman's seed, Jesus, would reverse their folly when the cross became our tree of life.

They were in fact made in the image of God but not equal to Him. The image of something speaks of a reflection, not an entirety. The serpent's deceptive rhetoric caused them to think they were receiving something when in actuality they were being stolen from. Rather than being enlightened, their understanding was darkened. This dragon spawn robbed them of their authority and position by pretending to befriend them. When deception speaks, you forget who you are and mistake enemies for allies.

Robbed of their immortality, their lives journeyed toward death and their light became shame. Dominion eroded into domination by the man and manipulation by the woman. The order of creation fell into chaos as multiplication gave way to division.

After this tumble, Adam named his wife Eve (*chava*) because she would be the mother of the human race. In a way, the woman's role was now her name.

Humankind suffered loss on every relational level. The intimate tie between man and woman was breached by division and distrust. This trickled down to loss in brother-to-brother and sister-to-sister relationships. The bond between parents and children was strained. The relationship between people and the earth was compromised. We need the gospel of hope and restoration to become a reality in every area that suffered loss. Jesus began the restoration process that we continue moving forward.

> For he must remain in heaven until the time for the final restoration of all things, as God promised long ago through his holy prophets. (Acts 3:21 NLT)

God created male and female with such an intimate connection that what wounds one wounds the other. And what heals one heals the other. Right now, both sexes/genders need healing.

I like to think of male and female as two sides of a rare coin. Each side of the coin bears a different image. For example, the American Gold Eagle has the head of a magnificent eagle on one side, and on the other side a glorious woman, a torch in one hand and a tree branch in the other. For the coin to hold its value, both sides must be in pristine condition. If either side is defaced, the value of the entire coin is diminished. In the same way, women will never increase their value by devaluing men any more than the worth of men will be raised by the oppressing of women.

The restoration of healthy relational dynamics between male and female will not happen by attacking and blaming males for the current woes, nor will it be healed by blaming women. The dragon is to blame. As we fight for our divine identity, we also fight for a return to the divine alignment of men and women.

———

What is one thing you can do to be part of the restoration of male and female?

What is one thing you can stop doing?

What is one thing you can pray?

CHAPTER 7

The Fight for Divine Alignment

If ever there comes a time when the women of the world come together purely and simply for the benefit of mankind, it will be a force such as the world has never known.

Matthew Arnold, British poet and philosopher

I still remember first reading this quote. My reaction was visceral. I felt the words enter my chest and reverberate throughout my being. I was shocked that a line written in the 1800s had lent both sense and reason to our moment in history. I may have cried. Something holy awakened. Questions raced through my mind. Was this possible? Could his words become a mandate for the women of our day?

For over a decade I've watched what happens when I share this quote. There is a collective gasp from the audience of women. Then phones appear to capture the words of the quote for themselves. If this resonated a decade ago, it should pierce our feminine hearts now.

But *if* is a tricky word pregnant with uncertainty.

If tells us a condition must be met in order for an event to occur.

This *if* is tied to a trifecta of time, pure motive, and women together.

This hope hinges on collective female voice and action. It could happen in our day. If we are free of offense and our motives are pure. The daughters of this age would need to gather in the hope of benefiting all.

This is not a question of *can we*; it is now a question of willingness. If we are willing, God is able. Long before a British philosopher suggested this, the Word of God prophesied it:

> Adonai gives the command;
> the women with the good news are a mighty army.
> (Ps. 68:12 CJB)

God is looking for the many women to have one voice. That at His word, they would declare the gospel, united in heaven's purpose. Unity of purpose works whether the intent is for evil or for good. We see this illustrated in Genesis 11, when a people united to build the tower of Babel.

> And the LORD said, "Behold, they are one people, and they have all one language, and this is only the beginning of what they will do. And nothing that they propose to do will now be impossible for them." (v. 6)

If God said nothing would be impossible for people who were united in rebellion, then how much is possible when godly women set their hearts on God's will for their lives and families?

When we gather in unity and in agreement with God's Word, it is blessed. Psalm 133:1–3 tells us that when brothers dwell in unity, there is a commanded blessing, and I believe the same applies to sisters. This focus is in line with our creative origins of flipping the "not good" dynamic of men alone to the "very good" dynamic of male and female together. This convergence of two who become one again in purpose and pursuit would yield a force previously unknown.

How many women would this require?

It Only Took Twelve

Jesus began His work of turning the world upside down with twelve men who were dedicated to the gospel. Those twelve discipled others until the good news of Jesus Christ reached the four corners of the world.

In recent history, twelve committed women adopted this strategy for very different reasons. Rather than coming together for the good of humankind, they united for the destruction of Western culture. The following is an excerpt from an article written by Mallory Millett, sister of radical second-wave feminist Kate Millett:

It was 1969. Kate invited me to join her for a gathering at the home of her friend, Lila Karp. They called the assemblage a "consciousness-raising-group," a typical communist exercise, something practiced in Maoist China. We gathered at a large table as the chairperson opened the meeting with a back-and-forth recitation, like a Litany, a type of prayer done in Catholic Church. But now it was Marxism, the Church of the Left, mimicking religious practice:

"Why are we here today?" she asked.

"To make revolution," they answered.

"What kind of revolution?" she replied.

"The Cultural Revolution," they chanted.

"And how do we make Cultural Revolution?" she demanded.

"By destroying the American family!" they answered.

"How do we destroy the family?" she came back.

"By destroying the American Patriarch," they cried exuberantly.

"And how do we destroy the American Patriarch?" she replied.

"By taking away his power!"

"How do we do that?"

"By destroying monogamy!" they shouted.

"How can we destroy monogamy?" . . .

"By promoting promiscuity, eroticism, prostitution and homosexuality!" they resounded.

They proceeded with a long discussion on how to advance these goals by establishing The National Organization of Women. It was clear they desired nothing less than the utter deconstruction of Western society. The upshot was that the only way to do this was "to invade every American institution. Every one must be permeated with 'The Revolution'": The media, the educational system, universities, high schools, K-12, school boards, etc.; then, the judiciary, the legislatures, the executive branches and even the library system.[1]

And there you have it.

With clarity and conviction, they were able to exceed their wildest dreams.

Twelve women began a revolution that successfully infiltrated every sphere of the American culture. Relentless and determined, they methodically sowed their message into and through every channel mentioned above. Division and discontentment spread through American households like a virus. The key to their successful cultural revolution was the systematic deconstruction of the family. And none of us should be surprised by their words. Kate Millett came out as a lesbian in 1970, identified as a bisexual during her twenty-year marriage to sculptor Fumio Yoshimura, then later married Sophie Keir.[2]

Feminists have always been open and honest about their goals. In 1970, activist Robin Morgan said, "We can't destroy the inequalities between men and women until we destroy marriage."[3]

And she was not alone in her thinking. Ms. magazine cofounder Gloria Steinem famously quipped a quote by Irina Dunn: "A

THE FIGHT FOR DIVINE ALIGNMENT

woman without a man is like a fish without a bicycle," which can be translated to mean that once again men are unnecessary. First there was a puncture that quickly grew into a rip. This tear in the fabric of the family began with an intimate breach between the man (referred to as the American Patriarch) and the woman. Notice that the way they proposed to *take away his power* was to remove the women from his "patriarchal" side. This meant dismantling marriage.

Rather than men being called fathers and husbands, they became "patriarchs" and oppressors. Labels work the magic of quickly fostering prejudice. Labels cause breeches that force people to choose sides. Labels depersonalize and lump individuals into a category of "all." That way the parts can become the hated whole. By assigning the attributes of some men to all men, all men became tyrants who oppress women. Feminists effectively downgraded the intimate alliance of husband and wife into the oppressor and the oppressed. Suddenly, women believed they were aiding and abetting their enemies (and some men were awful). Proving once again that "no city or house divided against itself will stand" (Matt. 12:25). Divided marriages gave way to divided households.

Monogamy was attacked strategically on both fronts. Men were told monogamy was impossible, and promiscuity was normalized. In 1968, theaters featured the first X-rated movie, and by 1975, *Playboy* magazine was the world's leading men's magazine. While men were outside the home living their best life, women were neglected and felt trapped at home with small children. This dynamic of unfaithful husbands and unfulfilled wives proved lethal to the family.

Feminists pounced on this betrayal. Gloria Steinem boldly declared that marriage itself was "the deprivation of a woman's civil rights."[4] Even though women had won the right to equal pay in 1963, and the Civil Rights Act of 1964 had confronted discrimination based on sex. But second-wave feminist leaders wanted more, and they entered the fray in the late 1960s with the goal of liberating women from the home.

The very hope of the aforementioned Marxist agenda.

The second-wave feminist movement differed vastly from previous women's groups that had focused on moral reform, abolition of slavery, the protection of family and biblical values, alcohol temperance, and the right of women of all colors and ethnicities to vote. In contrast, second-wave feminists pushed for greater access to abortion, reproductive freedom, and the deconstruction of the family. In the early 1970s, Phyllis Schlafly, a contemporary detractor of this agenda, warned that this would lead to a genderless society with the potential to devastate the family.[5] Her words were scorned at the time but have proved themselves tragically true in our day.

A new narrative was set in motion and reinforced by culture. Men were faithless tyrants and women the hapless victims desperate for liberation. Rather than demand better of men, we decided to join in with them. It was only fair that women should have the same sexual freedoms as men. With the advent of "the pill," they could!

I remember the shift. The tension in our home increased. My mother put a contract on the refrigerator that she had forced my father to sign. If he wasn't compliant with her demands by a certain date, she would take action and initiate a divorce. The messaging was everywhere. Men were put on notice. Women were breaking free from men. But were they getting free or exchanging one master for another?

Why would women possibly want to be home when they could be at the office earning money? Because work hours were nine to five, children were rushed off to school only to return to an empty house, and the latchkey generation was born. When John and I served as youth pastors in the late '80s, statistics cited the window after school from three to five p.m. as the most likely time for teens to engage in sex. Women and men returned home each night exhausted. Meals became rushed ordeals before spending a few short hours together and then hurrying children off to bed. With the majority of a family's waking life spent in school or at the office, home became the place to sleep rather than the place to live.

Here is the hard truth: the women's liberation movement wouldn't have been as successful as it was if the church had taught men and women how to live with and love one another well. The topic of submission in marriage has not always been presented in a healthy manner. Women are often subjugated rather than nurtured. John and I believe that marriage is two people committed to bringing out the best in one another. Scripture clearly instructs men how to lead like Jesus and warns them against the misuse of their position as husband and leader of the household. Scripture gives far more detailed instruction on how husbands are to conduct themselves than it does on the submission of wives. As the head of the household, the husband becomes the chief servant. Ephesians 5:28 says,

> In the same way [like Christ] husbands should love their wives as their own bodies. He who loves his wife loves himself.

Jesus modeled how the husband is to lead. Ephesians 5:22–33 reveals how Christ's pattern is reflected in the way men love their wives. When a man loves his wife, he is loving himself. Christ's love gives rather than takes and is committed to bringing out the best in His church. In the same way, a husband should lead in a way that brings out the best in his wife and family. Like Christ, husbands lead by example, *not* by intimidation or domination of any kind. Men who abuse their position of husband are the ones who are wrong, rather than the institution of marriage.

> Scripture gives far more detailed instruction on how husbands are to conduct themselves than it does on the submission of wives.

A glaring lack of this type of love helped the feminist movement gain traction, and people made the leap that the institution of marriage was flawed rather than the people involved. By making the exception the rule, women were encouraged to throw off the shackles of marriage and motherhood. Male and female together became "bad" rather than "good."

And Millett's word choice of "American Patriarch" has morphed into a byword commonly used to represent white males. Let's look a bit closer at this label. We know what *American* means, but what is the meaning of a patriarch? *Merriam-Webster* currently defines *patriarch* as "one of the scriptural fathers of the human race or of the Hebrew people," a "father or founder," and "the oldest member or representative of a group."[6] What I find curious is that since I began writing this book, the definition of *patriarch* has been edited. Rather than its current definition of "father or founder," it formerly was "the father and ruler of a family or tribe," and rather than "the oldest member or representative of a group," it was formerly "an old man deserving respect." These changes to the definitions are reflective of our current culture. But how did the God Most High describe Himself when He met with Moses?

> "I am the God of your father—the God of Abraham, the God of Isaac, and the God of Jacob." When Moses heard this, he covered his face because he was afraid to look at God. (Exod. 3:6 NLT)

God tied Himself to the Hebrews' patriarchal line. This does not mean women were unimportant or uninvolved, because without women there are no legacies. But He is God the Father, God the Holy Spirit, and Jesus is God the Son. God and Jesus are more than men, yet both are referred to with masculine designations: father, husband, brother, bridegroom, and son.

This raises another question. How can we be okay with the current denigration of the words *masculine* and *masculinity*? Neither are innately toxic, and yet the words *toxic* and *masculinity* have been paired so frequently, it is hard for some to imagine using one without the other. In a bold move away from "toxic masculinity," Gen Z women are referring to men of the more sensitive, submissive type as "so babygirl."[7] And what woman in her right mind would want to do life with a guy who behaves like a baby female?

Rather than pervert words or support toxic behavior, let's find ways to encourage men in *healthy masculinity*. This rarely comes by passing the definition through women first. Men are the ones who know the spectrum of what is healthy for biological males. When men are encouraged to act like women and women are encouraged to act like men, both genders move away from their positions of strength.

> Let's find ways to encourage men in **healthy masculinity**.

In the 1970s, respectful actions as innocent as men standing when a woman entered a room, pulling out women's chairs, or opening doors for women were perceived as insults. We declared we were more than capable of opening our own doors and pulling out our own chairs. All true, but these actions were never about our lack of strength, they were actions of respect and deference. Over the years, the number of men who open doors for women out of any formality of honor has plummeted.

What was *not* encouraged by the feminist movement was a healthy dynamic between males and females where both sexes won. It was the women's turn now! The option of godly marriages did nothing to further their cause. Examples of faithful men who loved, protected, nurtured, and provided for their wives and families were eliminated from their equations. But this is exactly how the healthy authority of a husband or father serves those under their care.

Husbandry is a term commonly used for the dressing and tending of grapevines to ensure their health and productivity. Psalm 128:3 describes healthy households in this way:

> Your wife will be like a fruitful vine
>   within your house;
> your children will be like olive shoots
>   around your table.

This beautifully describes a flourishing household. But when men dominate, their wives become diminished vines. In the battle of the sexes, both sides suffer loss, and like with most wars, both sides are wrong in some way. The imagery of women who forfeit their voices and dreams to the whims of selfish husbands and needy children is in stark contrast to Judeo-Christian values, which support women living full and fulfilling lives. Who could possibly forget the enviable woman of Proverbs 31 who bought a profitable field, planted a vineyard, produced linen, and sold it? She cared for those who sheltered in her household and provided for the poor and needy. She was freely empowered to flourish, and her husband praised and celebrated her success! Fulfillment comes when we reach beyond ourselves by a connection with the Giver of Life and touch the lives He wants to love through us.

A generation of women made the mistake of thinking "housewife" and "mother" were their identities when both were merely roles. In her book *The Feminine Mystique,* Betty Friedan pounced on the emptiness these women felt when surrounded by things but spiritually untethered. Rather than pursue a relationship with their Creator, women saw marriage and men as the problem. Interestingly, feminism rose to prominence alongside the Jesus movement. The answer women were looking for was spiritual renewal. But many latched on to feminism instead, which only exacerbated the problem.

As I have researched, I've begun to wonder if feminists have taken the words of Genesis more seriously than the church has. They understood that when men are alone, they are vulnerable and more easily corrupted. They knew the coupling of male and female was a power union that needed to be dismantled rather than healed. The devastation of marriage is not isolated to our United States.

Almost 90% of the world's population now live in countries with falling marriage rates. In the U.S., marriage has declined by 60% since the 1970s, while the median age for first marriages has increased for both men and women.[8]

A generation watched their parents' marriages disintegrate and decided marriages were nothing. I can't count the number of times I've been told by couples living together that marriage is only a piece of paper. They do not see marriage as a covenant between three: the man, the woman, and the God who makes the two one. Disappointed with their parents, they reject their parents' patterns. Rather than fight to build a healthy marriage, an ever-increasing number are refusing to marry. For many, this refusal means they will never become parents. Broken marriages beget broken children, and broken children become disenfranchised people.

Restoration and Rescue

Healthy cultures are built on and by healthy families. There are no perfect marriages or families, but all of us can learn how to do marriage and family in healthier ways. John and I are living proof to the truth that beautiful families can be born out of broken pasts.

One Christmas morning, I stood in awe of God's faithfulness. I watched as two couples in pajamas cuddled in my kitchen while the other two couples wrestled and played with my grandchildren in front of the Christmas tree. This was never my experience in my family of origin. There was a fight every Christmas. If someone didn't get what they wanted, we all paid. John and I decided to do Christmas with our family differently; our focus is on giving, not getting. In more ways than one, I resolved not to follow the unhealthy patterns of my parents, but rather than abandon marriage and family, we decided to build ours after God's pattern.

I believe the enemy's goal is to dismantle the family, therefore our goal should be to restore the family. We cannot trust this restoration to our government or culture because currently both have been influenced by the dragon. The prophet Isaiah spoke to the challenge of our day:

> Can plunder be retrieved from a giant,
>> prisoners of war gotten back from a tyrant?
>> (Isa. 49:24 MSG)

These are the questions I hear: Can our children be rescued? Can our marriages be restored? Can we recover the privacy and safety of our female spaces? Will our nation be spared? And God answers:

> But GOD says, "Even if a giant grips the plunder
>> and a tyrant holds my people prisoner,
> I'm the one who's on your side,
>> defending your cause, rescuing your children."
>> (v. 25 MSG)

God is always on the side of rescue.
God is always on the side of redemption.
God is always on the side of freedom from captivity.
God is always on the side of the oppressed and discouraged.

But once again it is crucial that we remember we are not wrestling with flesh and blood. We are in a cosmic wrestling match to rescue marriage and family. We fight *for* people. Let's review some of the tactics that brought us to the place where we are now so we can reverse engineer them:

Why are we here?
  To begin the restoration.
What kind of restoration?
  A spiritual restoration.
How does restoration start?
  By restoring the family.
How is family restored?
  Through rebirth and forgiveness.
How does this begin?
  It begins with me.

How will you start?
By honoring male and female.
How do we honor them?
By restoring dominion to both.
How do we do that?
By honoring God's design.
How do we honor God's design?
By protecting marriage and family.
How do we protect marriage and family?
By breaking partnership with darkness and pursuing Christ.

Healthy marriages are key because marriage is meant to reflect on earth the relationship of Christ and the church. Evil is best avoided by doing good and pursuing God. Holy intimacy in marriage with one is the opposite of the current trend of perverse promiscuity with many. Family matters because God is our Father, and we are all His children.

This battle will require more than legislation; it will be won through love and obedience. Under the banner of "Marks of the True Christian" in the ESV Bible, Romans 12:9 tells us,

Let love be genuine. Abhor what is evil; hold fast to what is good.

And here is the tension of our day. It is easy to abhor evil or to cling to what is good, but restoration and rescue require that we do both at once, and that is our challenge. Genuine love finds a way. This is the tightrope walk before each of us. It is always easier to abhor the evil we see in others while ignoring the evil that hides within us. *Abhor* is an intense word meaning "to regard with extreme repugnance: to feel hatred or loathing."[9] You'll never make excuses for the things you abhor.

I want to return to the powerful words of Matthew Arnold and invite you to hear them as if they were spoken just to you:

"If ever there comes a time." If not now, when?

"When women come together." Why not us?

Why don't we start this?

How much darker must it get? How much more must be stolen from our daughters before the evil of our day is confronted by our prayers and actions?

We need women of all ages, positions, races, and demographics. We need grandmothers, mothers, the single, the married, sisters, and daughters.

We need to come together, remembering the divine entrustments of womanhood: givers of life, tenders of wounds, providers of wisdom and kindness.

"For the benefit of mankind." In our day, it has become the *rescue* of mankind.

"It [the collective they] will be a force such as the world has never known." Yes—so be it.

———

What is one thing you can do to fight for divine alignment?

What is one thing you can stop doing in order to create more alignment between men and women?

What is one thing you can pray?

CHAPTER 8

The Fight for Truth

A lie doesn't become the truth, wrong doesn't become right, and evil doesn't become good just because it's accepted by the majority.

Booker T. Washington

I t was simply a photo, which I had uploaded on Instagram, of me in my car, wearing sunglasses and a T-shirt that read, "The Future Is Male and Female." My caption wasn't complicated. It read,

> The future is male and female because without male and female there is no future.

That was it. I kept it simple. I wasn't trying to be deep. I didn't think the sentiment was combative; it was biological reproduction. Admittedly the T-shirt was an expanded version of the more popular phrase "The Future Is Female."

The T-shirt had been given to me years ago at a women's conference. The statement honors the interdependent relationship between male and female. But by the reaction the post garnered on my social media, you would have thought it was revolutionary. Almost immediately I was called out.

Why would I want to minimize the oppression of women?

It was suggested this phrase was code for all lives matter; was I making a racial statement?

Had I been coerced into cosigning with patriarchy?

The anger in Christian women was palpable.

I was shocked by the leaps in logic. How did the future inclusion of males become an endorsement of any past oppression? Women continued to issue challenges in a similar tone. I had to ask myself, *Am I betraying females by standing up for males?* Economist Thomas Sowell posed a question we all must answer:

> Have we reached the ultimate stage of absurdity where some people are held responsible for things that happened before they were born, while other people are not held responsible for what they themselves are doing today?[1]

Yes, some men have oppressed women in the past. And yes, in some cultures men still oppress women, but that does not make all men oppressors. In my life, there have been both men and women who have played the role of competitor and detractor and both men and women who have encouraged me to be and do all that God created me to be and do. I bet most women in the Western world share my story. Including men in the future of humanity is not a play to unhealthy patriarchy. I love my brother, husband, sons, and grandsons. I cannot imagine life without them. I love the men on our team. I was not coerced to "cosign" on anything. I was incredulous. I thought we were women who preached inclusion rather than exclusion. Have we really become so bitter that we'd spew this type of inane stereotypical rhetoric? There is a win when both sexes are included. And a loss when either male or female is excluded.

The questions continued: Was my messaging about reproduction? Was I anti-LGBTQ+? First, to address the concept of reproduction, yes, male and female partner in the biological equation of future generations. Reproduction plays a major role, but that part or portion does not equal the whole of why male and female are both needed for a healthy future. And as far as anti-anything, whatever the letter, this thought was not why I had posted the photo.

A few women argued that men are automatically included, and therefore the mention of them now was unnecessary. Really? We live in a day when clarity is wisdom. How would women feel about T-shirts that read, "The Future Is Male"?

I think we'd counter there is no male without female!

Another defended "The Future Is Female" as a celebration of women coming up in the world. I was admonished not to coddle the men. That they (men) were the people of power. Does this make them worthy of our disdain? When did inclusion become coddling?

I was shocked at how a simple statement of biology and our reality for thousands of years had become so confusing. I was called a bigot for the first time. One man said my wearing a T-shirt that included both sexes made me a demon of hate. Another male assured me that the white males in the church didn't see me as their equal. Okay. I know who I am in Christ; I am a coheir, so it doesn't matter what others might think. I countered, "It's not about how they see me; it's about how I see them."

The vitriol was alarming.

Several women expressed their shock that such anger and hatred was levied by Christian women toward men. I've learned that when reactions are this charged, there is something more behind them. I saw the shadow of a dragon. I decided to pull back the curtain to see what I might find.

It wasn't hard. It was as simple as googling, "What is the origin of the quote, 'future is female'?"

Even I was surprised by the quote's origin. The slogan came from a 1970s school of feminist thought known as Labyris. These were lesbian separatists who promoted temporary or permanent lesbian isolation from men and heterosexuals. The name Labyris was adopted from the double-headed axe carried by the Amazons and Greek and Roman goddesses. The slogan "The Future Is Female" was part of a clothing presentation called "What the Well-Dressed Dyke Will Wear." It was printed on merchandise and sold in limited outlets to fund their mission.

Forty years later, feminists collaborated with the original creator of the merchandise, Liza Cowan, to reclaim the phrase. Branding was updated and widely marketed on clothing and other forms of merchandise, with 25 percent of the proceeds designated for Planned Parenthood. In her 2015 interview, Liza Cowan said, "The Future Is Female was a call to arms, an invocation . . . not just a slogan, but a spell." By 2017 the phrase was everywhere.[2] Today you can order unisex T-shirts emblazoned with the slogan, modeled by men, women, and children.

I asked a teenage boy what his thoughts were on the phrase. He paused then answered, "That I am unnecessary."

Social media is rife with interviewers asking women of all ages, "Are men necessary?" and every single one says no.

We may never be asked such a direct question, but I would hope we'd live in a way that clearly communicates that men are more than necessary, they are wanted. Toxic femininity is never the correct response to toxic masculinity.

Is this the messaging we want to send to our sons? Our grandsons? Our brothers? Our husbands? Our male friends? Our male coworkers, bosses, employees, or leaders? Men are struggling.

Their suicide rates are four times the rate of women's.[3] Millennials are more likely than previous generations to commit suicide, and the highest spike in suicide has been seen among males ages fifteen to twenty-four.[4] I am not okay with that. There is no denying that there is a male-hating spirit in play.

Having said all this, I understand there is also a female-hating spirit. I have been slandered and treated unfairly by Christian men. I am the first to acknowledge this, and much of our human history confirms that men are capable of horrible acts . . . but so are women. I have gone undercover in the brothels of India, Thailand, Cambodia, and Romania; I've seen the horrors of misogyny firsthand. And yet a number of the brothels I visited were run by madams. There will always be examples of the worst in countries that are overrun by poverty and by corruption. At the same time, history gives us examples of both noble men of valor and virtuous, wise women.

I've been hurt by men, but that doesn't mean I want to hurt and punish them. I've been wounded by women . . . repeatedly. Much of this is due to sin and the human experience. The whole of humanity is capable of unthinkably dark and inhumane things, but at the same time it is capable of the deeply empathetic and truly virtuous. Most days we live somewhere in between. It is the very reason we all—male and female, young and old—need the mercy of a Savior.

Embracing Female—or Erasing It?

When I first glanced at the group photo of the lesbian separatists from the 1970s, it would have been easy to mistake them for men. They had stripped themselves of every trace of femininity. Only hints of breasts gave them away. Which begs the question, Why would women emulate what they despised and sought to escape? Was it the men they hated, or the vulnerability of their womanhood?

In her compelling and thought-provoking book *The End of Woman*, Dr. Carrie Gress lends us this insight:

> Feminists have worked hard to mitigate women's suffering, but by trying to eliminate our vulnerability, by making us cheap imitations of men, and by ignoring our womanhood. Setting off in the wrong direction, the prescribed fix can't really fix anything. Instead, it has erased women one slow step at a time.[5]

She goes on to acknowledge that "instead of inspiring women to flourish as women and recognizing women's vulnerability, the goal has been to make women act, hope and dream like men."[6]

Tragically, by devaluing core female virtues, the feminists unwittingly set women up to be erased. After encouraging women to behave like men, it is understandable why feminists would find it difficult to call out men for presenting as women. Thus answering the question of why feminists' voices have been largely silent in the face of the "trans women are women" argument.

When J. K. Rowling dared to speak up, she was threatened with cancelation and labeled a TERF (trans-exclusionary radical feminist).

Writer Selwyn Duke warned, "The further a society drifts from the truth, the more it will hate those who speak it."[7]

In a world where there is no wrong, there can be no right. In a world where everyone has a different truth, there are no lies. The only wrong is saying there is wrong and right or truth and lies.

In days of confusion, living the "truth" is more powerful than speaking "truth." In response to a religion that preached truth without love, our culture now declares love without truth. But truth and love must coexist. God is love and truth. The two cannot be separated. One without the other twists both. Truth spoken but not lived is hypocritical and contradictory.

If you dare to speak the truth, you may be accused of hate. Just make sure the accusation isn't accurate. Jesus died for and loves all of us—even your accusers. Look beyond their reactions and speak the truth in love.

I remember there was so much anger when *Roe v. Wade* was overturned. One young girl lashed out at me and said I'd be dead soon and the decision would never affect me. I could have argued how it would affect my children and grandchildren. But when I paused and reread her words, what I saw was fear. So rather than defend my position, I spoke peace to her fears.

What Truth Is

After a long season of "my truth" and "your truth," let's revisit what truth is and is not. Truth is not an opinion, a feeling, or an experience. Truth is not limited to perspective. Truth is the whole rather than a fragment. Truth is more than fact and reality because truth has a transcendent eternal nature. As a follower of Jesus Christ, I believe He is the Truth. I believe the truth is a Who, not a what. He died so that we might know truth and experience true freedom and life in Him.

For generations, people have died for this belief; very few are willing to die for a lie. Lying is the dragon's language. He knows that lying unmakes us. The human body loses strength when it is in the embrace of a lie. Kinesiology, or muscle testing, has proved this to be true.[8] Once we are born again, lies are incompatible with the One who is truth. Truth is more than being truthful. It is lifting our soul and submitting our will to our Lord and Savior who is the Truth.

> Truth is not an opinion, a feeling, or an experience. Truth is not limited to perspective.

In *Common Sense*, philosopher and political activist Thomas Paine wrote, "A long habit of not thinking a thing wrong gives it a superficial appearance of being right."[9]

When lies are frequently repeated people begin to believe that falsehoods are true. But a lie repeated is nothing more than a lie multiplied. Frequency cannot make a lie a truth. A lie will always be a lie. And just as there is no agreement between daughters and dragons, there can be no agreement between lies and truth. Jesus is the Lord of truth and light; Satan is the dark lord of lies. There is no overlap. Lies are the shadowy covering that seeks to gaslight. Truth is the light that unveils right and good.

Choose Truth, Not Sides

We have been forewarned:

> But you need to be aware that in the final days the culture of society will become extremely fierce. People will be self-centered lovers of themselves and obsessed with money. They will boast of great things as they strut around in their arrogant pride and mock all that is right. They will ignore their own families. They will be ungrateful and ungodly. They will become addicted to hateful and malicious slander. Slaves to their desires, they will be ferocious, belligerent haters of what is good and right. (2 Tim. 3:1–3 TPT)

I believe the days of difficulty are here. Degradation always begins with a systematic undermining of structure and truth. John and I rarely get a "word," or what some call a prophecy, but when we do, they've been rather challenging. When we were in our early thirties, a minister called us out of a crowd and spoke this: "God is asking you to stand in the middle and declare truth, and because He has called you to do this, you will be shot at by both sides."

I thought, *Well, that sounds awful!* I didn't mind the first part, but the second half was daunting. Who wants to be shot at from

"God is asking you to stand in the middle and declare truth."

114

THE FIGHT FOR TRUTH

both sides? I was a young mother who wanted to be safe and fit in. Looking back over the last three decades of our life, I realize he wasn't wrong. And yet I wonder if this isn't a timely word for *all of us.*

> And if it is evil in your eyes to serve the LORD, **choose this day whom you will serve,** whether the gods your fathers served in the region beyond the River, or the gods of the Amorites in whose land you dwell. But as for me and my house, we will serve the LORD. (Josh. 24:15, emphasis added)

Choose you this day. Not a side, but a who you will serve. The Lord we choose determines the side we are on. There is no middle ground or Switzerland in the kingdom. A choice has to be made. If you refuse to choose who you will serve, the choice will be made for you.

Choosing sides is always easier. We are quick to believe the worst of one another and slow to believe the best. It's time we changed that. On the landmark weekend that *Roe v. Wade* was overturned, I was in Fort Worth at a large gathering of women who believed this ruling was an answer to prayer and something to celebrate. The thousand-plus women in this meeting wept, danced, prayed, repented, and cheered. I posted the eruption of praise to the only social media channel I interact with, Instagram, multiple times in both my feed and my stories. I flew home the next day, put down my phone, and focused on the wedding of my last son, his beautiful bride, and the friends and family who had flown in to celebrate with them.

But as we watched them exchange vows, a representative for godly womanhood pounced, slandering those who did not post to her preferred social media platform. I wasn't the only one she went after; she called out a number of female ministers. One was overseas and another was recovering from surgery.

Why am I mentioning this?

It's one thing for culture to behave in this divisive and destructive way but quite another when children of the kingdom act in this manner. Paul warned the Galatian church,

> But if you bite and devour one another, watch out that you are not consumed by one another. (Gal. 5:15)

It is better to close your mouth than to bite and devour. It's better to drop the stones and hit your knees. They are not my servants; they are God's and He knows how to deal with His servants. Rather than judge the motives of others, we all need to take a deep breath, pray, believe the best, and turn it over to the only One who truly knows their thoughts and intents. Let's choose truth rather than sides.

We see an interesting illustration of this in the book of Joshua. After forty years of wilderness wandering, the nation of Israel was on the threshold of entering their promised land. They had crossed the Jordan, made themselves ready, and were awaiting instructions on how to proceed. Joshua, their leader, was getting the lay of the land.

> When Joshua was by Jericho, he lifted up his eyes and looked, and behold, a man was standing before him with his drawn sword in his hand. And Joshua went to him and said to him, **"Are you for us, or for our adversaries?"** (Josh. 5:13, emphasis added)

I understand his question. I have asked it a hundred times myself! The children of Israel were coming out of a rough season. They'd been tricked, attacked by enemies, harassed by serpents and plagues, and beguiled by a corrupt prophet for four decades. The manna had stopped. The men were sore after being circumcised, and Israel was anxious to learn what they were up against. Joshua wanted to know whose side this guy was on. But listen to this man's response.

"Neither one," he replied. "I am the commander of the LORD's army."

At this, Joshua fell with his face to the ground in reverence. "I am at your command," Joshua said. "What do you want your servant to do?" (v. 14 NLT)

Rather than choose a side, he declared his alliance. I love this! He answered, "Neither one," as though to say, *Joshua, that's the wrong question! Rather than ask me about sides, ask me who I am; then you'll understand why I am here, and the time is now.* Forty years of nomadic wanderings had pruned and prepared a people ready to possess the soil of their forefathers. Joshua fell on his face and worshiped. When we find ourselves on holy ground, that is all we can do!

The commander of the LORD's army replied, "Take off your sandals, for the place where you are standing is holy." And Joshua did as he was told. (v. 15 NLT)

In a world promoting division, it's time we took off our shoes. We tread this earth on the threshold of a holy harvest. This coming season will involve both wheat and tares. Choose now and plant with care. Our words, deeds, and acts of kindness or cruelty become seeds that meet us in the future.

Redemption is possible when conflict is navigated in a godly manner. Rather than choose sides, we invite truth (Jesus) to be Lord over situations and conversations. When you read the Scriptures, you discover that Jesus refused to be entangled in fruitless religious arguments. Jesus loved the Pharisees, but He didn't let them derail Him. One way He accomplished this was by refusing to choose sides. When asked if it was lawful to pay taxes to Caesar, Jesus presented a coin and asked,

> Our words, deeds, and acts of kindness or cruelty become seeds that meet us in the future.

"Whose likeness and inscription is this?" They said, "Caesar's." Then he said to them, "Therefore render to Caesar the things that are Caesar's, and to God the things that are God's." (Matt. 22:20–21)

When they questioned His ethics and asked why Jesus ate with "tax collectors and sinners" He responded,

Those who are well have no need of a physician, but those who are sick. Go and learn what this means: "I desire mercy, and not sacrifice." For I came not to call the righteous, but sinners. (9:12–13)

This means that Jesus would eat with all of us because we have all sinned. His presence doesn't validate our sin. He joins us at our table to invite us to His Father's table.

Jesus loves justice, but when asked to settle a dispute, He went a bit deeper and reached for the heart of the matter.

Someone in the crowd said to him, "Teacher, tell my brother to divide the inheritance with me." But he said to him, "Man, who made me a judge or arbitrator over you?" And he said to them, "Take care, and be on your guard against all covetousness, for one's life does not consist in the abundance of his possessions." (Luke 12:13–15)

Covetousness can easily cloak itself to appear as justice. In this case, one brother felt that his portion of the inheritance was unfair. Jesus refused to get involved between the brothers. He spoke to the weightier matter, which was the protection of the man's heart.

Then there was the issue of someone who was not part of Jesus's inner circle casting out demons.

John said to him, "Teacher, we saw someone casting out demons in your name, and we tried to stop him, because he was not following us." But Jesus said, "Do not stop him, for no one who does a mighty work in my name will be able soon afterward to speak evil of me. For the one who is not against us is for us." (Mark 9:38–40)

I love this glimpse into John's humanity. He was frustrated that an outsider was using Jesus's name! They tried to shut him down, but it didn't work. Jesus assured John that even though the guy was not "one of them," he was one in purpose with them!

Jesus loved His disciples, but when they wanted to call down fire on a city that did not receive Him, they got rebuked.

And when His disciples James and John saw this, they said, "Lord, do You want us to command fire to come down from heaven and consume them, just as Elijah did?"

But He turned and rebuked them, and said, "You do not know what manner of spirit you are of. For the Son of Man did not come to destroy men's lives but to save them." And they went to another village. (Luke 9:54–56 NKJV)

This interaction is a warning to all. Even when there is scriptural precedent, we can be influenced by the wrong spirit. Once again proving that all of us can end up being terribly wrong when we think we are right. Why would anyone think calling for the destruction of the people our Lord sent us to rescue is a good idea? It is like burning down a prison without first saving the prisoners.

Jesus loved the Samaritans, but rather than getting entangled with the concept of where to worship, He shared the secret of how to worship.

But the hour is coming, and is now here, when the true worshipers will worship the Father in spirit and truth, for the Father is seeking such people to worship him. God is spirit, and those who worship him must worship in spirit and truth. (John 4:23–24)

In each situation, we must ask ourselves, *Am I choosing sides or am I choosing Spirit and truth? Am I rescuing or provoking?* I know I am asking a lot of you, but there is so much at risk if we don't do this well. Rather than hone our arguments, let's pray for a greater sensitivity to the Holy Spirit. The dragon has decreed death over this generation—let's stand in the middle and speak truth and life.

Let's pray and ask God for His wisdom.

Heavenly Father,

We come to You for wisdom. Your Word says in James 1:5, "If any of you lacks wisdom, let him ask God, who gives generously to all without reproach, and it will be given him." We need Your wisdom. Thank You for an abundant outpouring of Your holy insight. We need the help and counsel of Your Holy Spirit. Thank You for the promise of the Spirit of truth. Reveal any area in our lives where we have chosen sides rather than love and truth.

———

What is one thing you can do to fight for truth?

What is one thing you can stop doing?

What is one prayer you can pray?

CHAPTER 9

The Fight to Find Your Voice

Some people's idea of free speech is that they are free to say what they like, but if anyone says anything back, that is an outrage.

Winston Churchill

Recently I reposted a short film that captured the angst of female athletes who have trained and competed with females but are being forced to compete against biological males. It was the beautiful story of how a father nurtured his daughter's dream to be the fastest woman alive. As he watched his daughter train relentlessly, this father declared, "Ain't no woman alive that can beat you!"

After years of training and dreaming, she discovered her efforts were in vain. The rules had changed, and she was now competing against a biological male who identified as a woman.[1]

The short video was followed by several accounts of females who'd been displaced by biological males in athletic competitions.

The video contained no judgment. There was no mention of sin. It did not incite hate or violence. There was no call to action. It wasn't a Christian video. It was created by a watch company to highlight the current inequity in competitions. It was thought-provoking and professional. I reposted it with this caption:

Use your voice and keep your daughter's dreams alive.

I hoped mothers would advocate on behalf of their daughters and get involved with local athletic programs. I hoped they would see what was at risk. Many mothers and former athletes did. But the reactions of several biological women surprised me. They thought I'd stepped out of line. Their anger with me far exceeded any empathy they might have for these injustices.

The kinder ones told me to use my platform only to preach the gospel, while the angrier end of the spectrum accused me of being transphobic, manipulative, and afraid of science. I was threatened with the judgment of God. They lashed out from private accounts and judged me for blocking them. Which is ironic, because they obviously weren't blocked, or they wouldn't have been able to read my post or leave comments. Most of their rage was not about the impossibility of fair competition between biological women and men. Instead, there were heated opinions about my opinion. And because we didn't see things the same way, a diatribe was unleashed in an effort to shame me into a quiet corner.

You've probably realized that you are free to parrot but not to protest. When *everything* is *right, nothing* can be called *wrong.* Only those who believe there is right and wrong are allowed to be labeled wrong. They will always be wrong when wrong is right.

If you say something as logical as "Men shouldn't compete in women's sports," you'll hear comments like, "God loves everyone." Which, of course, He does. But that is completely off topic. What does the love of God have to do with male athletes injuring or displacing females in women's sports? Absolutely nothing.

What the film pointed out, and I affirmed, is that trans women have all the physical advantages of males. Biological men have an average of 36 percent more muscle mass than females; conversely, women normally have twice, and sometimes three times, the fat percentage of males. Men develop larger bones and have higher peak bone mass than women. Men have an average of six inches of height over women, but many men have more than a foot in height differential. When it comes to strength, men are larger and stronger than women. Men have on the average twenty-six more pounds of skeletal muscle, 40 percent more upper body strength, and 33 percent more lower body strength than women of the same fitness level.[2]

We have seen this dynamic of physical superiority play out as trans women are allowed to compete in formerly all-female athletic competitions. Recently, a freshman boy, ranked 172nd in a cross-country meet, trans-identified and is now the "fastest sophomore girl" at the same regionals, beating the closest biological girl by ninety-eight seconds.[3]

"Trans women" are Amazonian compared to biological women. But in many cases, these are intact males who have taken advantage of the struggle of the truly gender dysphoric for their own gain.

Recently the coach of a girl's high school basketball team forfeited the game when three of his players were injured by a six-foot trans woman playing on the opposing team. In the video from the game, I watched as these girls were tossed about like rag dolls. One of the three girls was writhing in pain.[4] How has this happened? Why are parents allowing this injustice to be done to their daughters? I would suggest it starts with the role social media now plays in our lives.

Circuses, Spectators, and the Powers That Be

In December 2019, I wandered the Roman Colosseum with my oldest son, Addison, and his lovely wife, Julianna. The wind was biting, and we rushed from one patch of sun to the next to escape the morning chill as our tour guide explained the Colosseum's history. I'd heard this dialogue before, so I allowed my mind to wander. In many ways, it's unfathomable that a culture advanced enough to build the Flavian Amphitheatre debased themselves by how they chose to use it.

At one time, this architectural masterpiece held an estimated audience of fifty thousand people. Admission was free, and the events drew people from every social stratum of the Roman Republic. Designated entrances guided the citizenry to the seating for their social class. The masses gathered to watch gladiators wound, maim, and kill animals or one another. These spectacles of cruelty continued for centuries until the emperor Honorius I ended the games in AD 404.

Not far from the Colosseum lie the ruins of the Circus Maximus. It predates the Colosseum and was Rome's largest public venue, accommodating one hundred and fifty thousand spectators. The Circus hosted chariot races, Roman games, and gladiator bouts. The Circus Maximus is where Paul was beheaded and Peter was crucified upside down. It was there that Nero martyred Christians to deflect personal blame for the fires of Rome. Tacitus wrote in his *Annals*,

> Therefore, to stop the rumor [that he had set Rome on fire], he [Emperor Nero] falsely charged with guilt, and punished with the most fearful tortures, the persons commonly called Christians. . . . A vast multitude were convicted, not so much on the charge of burning the city, as of "hating the human race."[5]

Nero had a crisis; fire had ravaged ten of Rome's fourteen districts. He needed a scapegoat. Roman Christians were an easy target because they did not partake in the debauchery of the Roman culture. Nero accused and arrested the Christians. After they were tortured, their bodies were set on fire as lights for the Circus. What began with a crisis (the fire), morphed into a wholesale hatred and persecution of beliefs. Throughout the Roman Empire, the Christians and Jews who dared to live separate from the Roman *culture* were accused of hate. Roman poet Juvenal suggested that if people are given "bread and circuses," they'll be satisfied.[6] Before we imagine that this type of corruption, perversion, and bloodshed could never happen in a democratic nation, remember that Rome was a republic. Let's step back and look at the parallels.

In addition to Christians being currently labeled as hateful bigots, an anti-Semitic spirit has raised its ugly head again. Our streets and college campuses resound with threats of violence. For nearly two decades, social media has given a voice to the masses. With nearly five billion users, the venue of social media has exceeded the combined capacity of the Circus Maximus and the Colosseum twenty-five thousand times over. The online world has become an event space for every kind of spectacle. It is the public forum where trials are held and victims and victors are made.

Social media is not a place we go; it's a world we carry. But has any of this made us kinder, braver, or more compassionate? Unfortunately, no. The data shows us we are less confident and less connected than ever. Vast networks challenge intimate connections. It is easier to argue with strangers than navigate hard conversations at home. We are at once overwhelmed by social media and underwhelmed by our lives.

In recent years, we've seen up close what should have only been seen at a distance. We feel responsible and accountable for things outside our control or authority to change. Every day we are presented with more problems than answers. The constant inundation is exhausting, and people spiral into depression and anger.

The circus has not come to town; the circus *is* our town.

We've passively watched as an assortment of clowns, acrobats, tightrope walkers, jugglers, magicians, and bearded ladies invaded our homes. The circus has interrupted our workplaces, undermined our schools, and mocked our houses of worship.

Nero canceled the Christians, and the Nazis canceled the Jews. Once a people group is cut off from their community, their destruction becomes easy. Roman and German citizens watched as their neighbors were stripped of their dignity and livelihood. They saw acts of inhumanity up close; we watch through a screen and run an even greater risk of becoming spectators.

Imagine how the victims in the Circus Maximus felt surrounded by an arena of people who could have overwhelmed Nero's actions by virtue of their numbers. What if everyone had refused to show up at the Colosseum or the Circus? Perhaps it would not have taken four hundred years to shut down the games. But that didn't happen. Even if the Romans didn't like what they witnessed, they ate their bread and watched, thankful it wasn't happening to them. The cruelty and injustice we tolerate for others will eventually overtake us all. Holocaust survivor and Nobel laureate Elie Wiesel wrote,

> What hurts the victim most is not the cruelty of the oppressor, but the silence of the bystander.[7]

How many times must we hear this before we believe it? I've watched people I respect cower under the accusing voice of a few because the many refused to speak up for them. Let's not agree in theory but not be supportive of one another in reality. A theory of agreement is useless. I understand—silence is easier. Intimidation is a wildly successful tool, which is the reason it is so widely utilized. Don't let intimidation shrink your life and limit your voice.

Don't let intimidation shrink your life and limit your voice.

A Double-Edged Sword

Females of all ages are being threatened by a double-edged sword. One edge is the systematic sexualization of female; the other is the silencing of women. As culture sexualizes women, there are those in the church working hard to silence females. Tragically, the church should be helping her daughters find and refine their feminine voice. God would never have given us a voice if He intended for us to remain silent. I understand that some women have misused their voices, but there are men who have done the same. Help women find their voice and use it in the right way and for the right reasons. No one has the right to steal the voices of our daughters. This is not an invitation to use our voices against others. It is a call to recover our voices on behalf of women. This is not about placing blame—it's about taking back our place.

So where do we go from here?

Our sons and daughters need us to advocate. Our nation needs us to pray. Our families need to heal. Our husbands need our respect. People need our love.

We need to remember what it means to be a woman. We cannot continue to be those who simply watch. As one philosopher quipped,

No snowflake in an avalanche ever feels responsible.[8]

If the proverb "People follow courage" is true, let's give others examples to follow and not live ensnared by the opinions of strangers. I believe we begin to recover our voice by having conversations with real, live people. Far too many women have lost their voices. I understand that some conversations are difficult if you don't know who is in the room. Social media is rarely a safe space. But what about in your home, at your church, or in a Bible study group? To this end, I've hosted online and in-person intensives so people could ask questions and talk in rooms without fear. There is so much conflicting information and confusion around the issue of what it means to be a female. Sometimes you find your voice by simply saying no.

Just Say No

A simple no without any clarification or justification.

No to unhealthy people and practices allows a yes to healthy ones.

No to unwise choices makes a way for wiser ones.

No to ignorance is a yes for knowledge.

No one has the right to take away your no; our all-powerful God empowers us to make choices.

If you're not free to say no, you were never free to say yes. Conversely, if you are only free to say yes, then you never had a choice. The current dynamic of freedom of speech is permission to echo.

Disagreeing doesn't mean you're hateful any more than agreeing means you're loving. You have every right to say no to the unreasonable and the abusive.

No to the Unreasonable

In 2021, I traveled solo on a short Southwest flight that was nearly empty. I chose a window seat near the front and settled in. It wasn't long before a woman chose the aisle seat. There was an open seat between us, and I invited her to utilize the storage space under that seat for her bag. She thanked me.

"Of course," I replied.

She recognized my voice. Which was the only way she could have possibly guessed who I was because we both had masks on our faces.

"Are you Lisa?"

"I am."

She introduced herself and let me know she'd heard me minister a few times. We started up a conversation. She was a fellow Italian traveling home after a troubling visit with her father in Chicago. She was exhausted and concerned for her parents.

After a while, our conversation took on a lighter tone and we laughed about the crazy dysfunctions of an Italian upbringing. We weren't loud, but we were happy. That was when the woman in the row behind us shook our seats and told us to shut up. My seatmate froze midsentence and ducked. I was surprised, but I didn't duck. I turned around, looked over the seat at the woman, and replied, "No."

This was one of the first times since the pandemic that I'd experienced any measure of joy, conversation, or connection on a flight. And I certainly wasn't going to allow one angry woman to take it away from us. My Italian sister was shocked.

I volunteered, "You can use headphones or move to another seat. This flight is wide open and there are plenty of available seats."

Well, she was not having it. She'd forgotten her headphones and was traveling with friends, so she wasn't moving. We dropped our voices and continued our conversation.

She shook our seats again and yelled, "Shut up!"

Her aggression was palpable. I noticed she was a large woman, crammed into the middle seat between two blissfully unaware women watching movies.

"No," I calmly repeated as I turned around.

She pitched a fit. She yelled how selfish, uncaring, and rude I was. At this point the flight attendant came on the scene.

"Is there a problem?" she asked.

"She wants us to stop talking," I explained.

"Well, you don't have to," the flight attendant assured us.

The angry woman went silent. When we deplaned, my new friend stayed by my side, afraid the woman might try to fight me.

For the record, I fly all the time. This wasn't a night flight with people sleeping, and it was an hour in duration. Her request was unreasonable. It wasn't our fault she'd forgotten her headphones and refused the option of moving to another seat. You have every right to say no to the unreasonable.

No to the Abusive

When women are silent about the small things, it is almost impossible to be vocal on the bigger issues. Over the years I've heard far too many stories of girls who were sexually or emotionally abused by fathers, brothers, or family friends. In almost every case, either their mothers didn't believe them or they knew what was happening but didn't protect them. Some of these mothers were so broken themselves that they didn't know what to do. Others were afraid that doing something would be too costly. If the mothers had been victims of abuse, they often felt powerless. They had failed to protect themselves and failed to protect their daughters.

Then there is a more twisted than broken version: mothers who'd rather protect their image than their daughters. They are those who hide or downplay abuse. In a recent documentary, the parents of two daughters who had been sexually abused by their brother played it off as curiosity that happened when the girls were asleep. This type of cowardice must stop. I understand that confronting any type of abuser is frightening. I can't begin to imagine the heartbreak of sexual abuse of any child in a family. But another generation of children shouldn't be enslaved by the chains of our past. This fight for female means we no longer make excuses for any type of abuse. Mothers protect their daughters, even if it means exposing their husband, their son, or any other family member or friend.

How to Lovingly Disagree

Not long ago, my favorite hairdresser disappeared. I'd gone to him for years and treasured our friendship. He had shared portions of his personal life and challenges with me. I knew that he had a boyfriend and that they had both grown up in the church.

When I couldn't reach him through the salon, I texted him to see if he was okay; thankfully he was. I asked where he'd gone and why he hadn't told me. He explained that he was transitioning to a woman and knew I wouldn't agree with his choice. I let him know that the fact that I'd been married for four decades proved that I could love someone I didn't always agree with. I do not believe disagreement in one area should mean a broken relationship in all areas. I made an appointment. When we were face-to-face, I shared my concern that he was making an irreversible decision that might not solve his longings for love and that he might come to regret it later. He heard me and I heard him. Nothing but friendship passed between us, and I continued to visit him until I moved.

As an author and female minister, I'm friends with people who disagree with me. Disagreement shouldn't mean alienation and hate. Friendships and marriages are built on mutual respect rather than total agreement. I've had innumerable conversations on flights with complete strangers on everything from religion to politics. We rarely agree on everything. But at the end of the flight, we shake hands and more often than not exchange contact information. If that can happen between strangers, it should be able to happen between family and friends. When people are heard and respected, conversations become gifts that help us think, grow, and learn even if we still disagree. Part of finding our voice is offering people friendship.

> Don't buy the lie that disagreement equals hate.

Over the course of our marriage, John and I have disagreed on several things. Some of these are things we now agree on, but there are other issues that we may never agree on. But that does not change our commitment to one another. Neither of us is willing to lose our relationship to win an argument. Don't buy the lie that disagreement equals hate.

Don't let disagreements make you an enemy. Keep pressing in with kindness.

But if you can't disagree in a loving, respectful manner, push the pause button. We want people to hear us, not be hurt by us. We need a spirit of love and truth. People have questions that require honest but loving answers. Jesus models this for us in Mark 10:21.

> And Jesus, looking at [the rich young man], loved him, and said to him, "You lack one thing: go, sell all that you have and give to the poor, and you will have treasure in heaven; and come, follow me."

Jesus looked, listened, and loved this man before speaking to him. He exposed the one thing that had trapped the young man while at the same time inviting him into the freedom of generosity. Jesus knew the obstacle that stood between the two of them walking forward together. The man went away sad, but Bible scholars believe he returned later as a disciple. Hard truths and hard turns are always easier when the dynamic of love is in play. Often, the "one thing" is not the obvious one. My one thing shifted when I experienced God's mercy and love, knowing I deserved His judgment. I believe people ultimately want to belong. We seek alignment with the lesser when we fear our longing for the higher is impossible. We settle for aligning with culture but are desperate for an alignment with heaven. We were each created for a God-aligned identity. Again, we see spirit and truth in operation in John 3:16–17:

> For God so loved the world, that he gave his only Son, that whoever believes in him should not perish but have eternal life. For God did not send his Son into the world to condemn the world, but in order that the world might be saved through him.

God gave His Son so we could identify with His Son. He gave when all we knew to do was take. He turned His face toward us long before we turned to Him. Our Father gave His only begotten

Son when we were yet enemies. It was the kindness of God that led most of us to repentance.

It is now courageous to say women are biological females. It shouldn't be, but suddenly it is. You'll be accused of gaslighting, judging, shaming, unfounded phobias, privilege, and hatred. It is your responsibility to make sure that none of these accusations are true. If we are not careful, we can be right in the wrong spirit. Hate is easier than love. Pride is easier than humility. Kindness will require effort; cruelty comes to us quicker. Guarding your heart is more important than engaging in an argument. When you're called out for things you didn't do, don't call them out on things they've done. Disciples of Christ don't slap back. James 1:19 tells us,

> Understand this, my dear brothers and sisters: You must all be quick to listen, slow to speak [or post], and slow to get angry. (NLT)

A quick response might be your worst course of action. I've learned this lesson the hard way. Here are some other options instead.

Exit the Room

Disengage. Take a deep breath, put down the phone, close the computer, and simply walk away. Online crazy is easier to disengage from. No one is forcing you to make the comment, so don't. If it is an in-person conflict, get a drink of water, go to the bathroom, or calmly announce you're stepping away. Leaving the room changes the dynamic. You don't storm out, and there is no yelling from the kitchen! Your home is your real world; the phone is the pretend one. Words are fuel for both real and online fires. Cut off the kindling.

> For lack of wood the fire goes out,
>   and where there is no whisperer, quarreling ceases.
>   (Prov. 26:20)

Away from the chaos, your chances of hearing from the Holy Spirit will be better. It is okay to excuse yourself from any conversation to meet with the Counselor. You have permission to turn off your social media for a few days. Do not let trolls and strangers rob you of your peace. If for some reason a social media exit is not an option, remember, it is your page and everyone else on it is a guest. You have every right to restrict or block combative or hateful guests. You can delete and disable comments. And for your soul's sake, stay away from combative threads. This will help prevent you from wasting time arguing and free you up for real conversations.

Social media is full of trolls who love to create chaos. Some want to scam you for money. Others want to rob you of your emotional energy. Do not engage with them. Dragons and trolls love to waylay you with outrageous lies tethered to tiny bits of truth.

Their ultimate goal is to wound your spirit. Your heart is more important than your reputation. Don't compromise your heart. The Holy Spirit will empower you to show love in the face of hate and be fearless in the face of threats. But even David walked away when Saul started throwing spears. Here is a Scripture to keep in mind as you recover your voice:

> Let the words of my mouth and the meditation of my heart
> be acceptable in your sight,
> O LORD, my rock and my redeemer. (Ps. 19:14)

Stand Up for and with Others

I had two of my granddaughters over for dinner. I love that I can do this. Earlier that week, my son had shared that a boy had made a mean comment to one of them. Over dinner, we talked about it. I told her I'd had a similar experience at her age. But there was a big difference between her story and mine. I was devastated, but she was barely fazed. Before she could answer him, another girl in her class told the bully that he was wrong. May we emulate the courage of that child. Calling a bully a bully doesn't stop their actions, but speaking the truth will.

Your voice is your first line of defense, which is why the enemy wants it silenced. When a woman is attacked, the last thing her attacker wants is for her to scream. I'm not asking you to scream, but it's time you escape any prison of silence. Maybe you never lost your voice but out of frustration have been misusing it. I personally have been guilty of both. We can no longer afford to be careless, silent, or misdirected. The fight for female is a commitment to use our voice and choices in constructive ways on behalf of both men and women. You don't have to attend the social circus. Let's speak so we can be heard. I believe this begins with how we speak to one another. We can disagree without yelling.

Up until now we've addressed interacting with people. Now let me share with you the secret of where your voice is the most productive. It's the most powerful when lifted in prayer.

> In every place of worship, I want men [and women] to pray with holy hands lifted up to God, free from anger and controversy. (1 Tim. 2:8 NLT)

I know this verse specifies *men*, but I am sure Paul wanted women to pray as well. Hands lifted to God is a posture of surrender. It also symbolizes transferring everything to God. I've prayed angry prayers before; they usually involve my will or frustration. God can sort through our nonsense, but anger never brings out the best in anyone. Another word for *controversy* is *argument*. God wants the disputes between us settled so He can work through us. Rather than denouncing one another, let's believe the best and announce God's faithfulness.

> First of all, then, I urge that supplications, prayers, intercessions, and thanksgivings be made for all people, for kings and all who

are in high positions, that we may lead a peaceful and quiet life, godly and dignified in every way. (1 Tim. 2:1–2)

We don't pick and choose who we pray for. We don't just pray for some people, or our people; we have the privilege of praying for all people. When womanhood is up for grabs, our children and nation need healing. Confession and healing begin with us. James 5:16 says,

> Confess your sins to each other and pray for each other so that you may be healed. The earnest prayer of a righteous person has great power and produces wonderful results. (NLT)

The New King James Version tells us "the effective, fervent prayer of a righteous man avails much." Fervent prayer is scriptural prayer. There is nothing more powerful than praying and singing God's words. We shouldn't allow culture to form our prayers when God has given us kingdom prayers. One of the prayers Jesus models for us is in Luke 11:2–4. The New Living Translation reads,

> Jesus said, "This is how you should pray:
>
> "Father, may your name be kept holy.
>   May your Kingdom come soon.
> Give us each day the food we need,
> and forgive us our sins,
>   as we forgive those who sin against us.
> And don't let us yield to temptation."

The King James Version takes it a bit further:

And he said unto them, When ye pray, say, Our Father which art in heaven, Hallowed be thy name. Thy kingdom come. Thy will be done, as in heaven, so in earth.

Give us day by day our daily bread.

And forgive us our sins; for we also forgive every one that is indebted to us. And lead us not into temptation; but deliver us from evil.

And in Matthew 9:37–38, we're told,

Then he [Jesus] said to his disciples, "The harvest is plentiful, but the laborers are few; therefore pray earnestly to the Lord of the harvest to send out laborers into his harvest."

The enemy always attacks right before the harvest because he wants to steal God's harvest of souls. Prayer is a privilege, and we need the prayers you will voice.

What is one area where you've lost your voice?

What is the one thing you can do to recover it?

What is one prayer you can pray?

CHAPTER 10

The Fight for Common Sense and Common Language

A society is in decay, final or transitional, when common sense really becomes uncommon.

G. K. Chesterton

Recently, I babysat four of my grandchildren for eight days while their parents visited the United Kingdom. It rained every single day, which created lots of opportunities for conversations with the two boys and two girls who ranged in age from five to twelve. At one point my seven-year-old grand-daughter shared how a former neighbor named Sara had cut her hair, changed schools, and would now be a boy named Sam.

I posed a question, "What if I put on a giraffe suit and said I was a giraffe? Would that make me one?"

She made a face and countered, "You're too short to be a giraffe." She's not wrong.

I pivoted. "What if I identified as a short giraffe?"

"That's just silly!" she asserted.

"So, does cutting her hair make her a boy?" I asked.

She paused, thought a moment, and answered, "No."

"Why not?" I questioned.

"You know why," she whispered.

"No, why?" I insisted.

She motioned to her nether region and asserted, "Her bottom!"

I left the conversation there. We didn't discuss DNA or the nuances of gender versus biological sex. I worked with the details she provided because that was what she was comfortable with. There was no need for me to sexualize or emotionally charge the conversation. I assumed she'd already spoken with her parents and knew the answer before she broached the conversation. She was testing me. But never in my wildest dreams did I imagine I'd have this conversation with a seven-year-old.

Let's start with a definition:

common sense, noun: sound and prudent judgment based on a simple perception of the situation or facts.[1]

I find it interesting that the synonyms for *common sense* include *discretion, wisdom, prudence, sensibleness,* and *sense*. Another way to look at this word is a sense that is held in common or generally agreed upon.

Voltaire bemoaned, "Common sense is very rare."[2]

And more's the pity. Nonsense is increasingly accepted as the norm. But when words are constantly changing, the ground beneath our feet keeps shifting. We have wandered far off the beaten path and lost some of our sense of direction. Which is a bit precarious because in life and on highways, guardrails prove helpful. For time beyond reckoning, binaries have helped us measure the boundaries of life. Harvard-educated attorney Phyllis Schlafly made this point in August 2016:

> Anyone with a child knows that children learn about the world through binary options: up or down, hot or cold, big or little, inside or outside, wet or dry, good or bad, boy or girl, man or woman. But the radical feminists, who staff women's studies departments at most colleges, have propagated the idea that we have to get rid of the "gender binary" along with the expectation of distinct roles for men and women.[3]

And though you may not agree with all her political views, her cautionary statement has proven itself to be true. Can we all agree that concepts like up or down, left or right, and hot or cold are helpful, not harmful? Why would radical feminists want to replace the common sense of gender binary with an ever-expanding nonbinary? When you undermine commonly held beliefs, you're positioned to deconstruct the foundations of a culture.

We grow the most by learning *how* to think rather than being told *what* to think. Information is useless if we lack context, insight, and common sense. One of the cruelest things we can do is cause our children to doubt themselves, even as we strip ourselves of common sense. We hear so much about healthy boundaries, yet are we allowing a confused culture to overrun the guardrails of common sense and our children?

If we will not stand up for our children, then they will have to stand up for themselves. The poem "I Am Not a Dress" was written and performed by a fourteen-year-old Irish girl to combat the nonsense she encountered. It went viral online, and I've excerpted a few lines here:

> We are women, we are warriors of steel
> Woman is something no man will ever feel
> Woman is not a skill that any man can hone
> Woman is our word and it is ours alone

> I am not a dress to be worn on a whim
> A man in a dress is nonetheless a him
> Women are not simply what we wear
> If this offends you, I do not care.[4]

Her entire poem is worth reading. What she shared is the beautifully crafted cry of our daughters. I understand it was published under a pseudonym to protect her and her family from backlash. Where is her right to free speech?

If even the beloved author and billionaire J. K. Rowling was attacked for saying, "If [biological] sex isn't real, the lived reality of women globally is erased,"[5] what type of backlash would a young Irish girl face? It's a sad day when the common sense of a child is more accurate than the perspective of an educated adult. How has this happened? When we turn from God, we lose touch with ourselves. Our real, beautiful, feminine selves. We are far more than what we've pretended to be. The current famine of common sense and meteoric rise of foolishness are intricately connected with our spiritual decline.

> Yes, they knew God, but they wouldn't worship him as God or even give him thanks. And they began to think up foolish ideas of what God was like. As a result, their minds became dark and confused. Claiming to be wise, they instead became utter fools. (Rom. 1:21–22 NLT)

We are a nation with confused ideas about God, which has led to confused ideas about ourselves. Romans goes on to say,

> Since they thought it foolish to acknowledge God, he abandoned them to their foolish thinking and let them do things that should never be done. (1:28 NLT)

When this type of foolishness has taken hold of a people, or a nation, God abandons them to their own devices. A culture in this state of abandonment imagines their foolishness to be wisdom.

Common Sense and Compassion

A few months after my babysitting adventure, my older grand-daughter brought up the same issue. For years, she'd known the young girl as Sara. One day, she'd knocked on the neighbors' door and asked if Sara could play.

The father yelled, "The name is Sam, not Sara!" and slammed the door in her face. My granddaughter was confused by the dad's anger. She thought her friend was gender fluid and could go by both names.

"What's her home life like?" I asked. "Are her parents together?"

She explained that the parents had recently divorced.

"She's probably hurting," I volunteered.

"Yes, that is what my parents said," she answered.

The fact that this young girl's world had been turned upside down might have been reason enough for her to feel the need for a new identity. Perhaps she hoped it would win her parents' notice and protection or grant her a sense of belonging amid a divided and turbulent family situation. I don't know, but I understand the trauma of divorce.

My parents announced their divorce as I entered middle school. Their split knocked my whole world sideways. My grades plummeted, my friendships changed, and my behavior became erratic. I lost my bearings because I didn't know what or who to believe in. I was an awkward teen draped in loose overalls to hide my lack of feminine form. I'd hate to think what might happen if I was attending public school today. If it had been suggested that I was born in the wrong body, I probably would have agreed with them. *Everything* else in my life felt terribly wrong; why would I think my body was right? If I'd been asked to self-identify when I was in junior high, I would have said I was a unicorn. It certainly felt like I had more in common with a mythical creature than the girls in my gym class. But feelings are not facts.

I thank God I was protected from making life-defining choices during the most vulnerable time of my life. The adults in my world assured me the awkwardness of adolescence would pass. If I'd believed that I was in the wrong body, I would have missed out on so much in my life that later proved beautiful and right. If I'd believed my *then* was my forever, I might have lost hope. My future held more than an adolescent girl from a broken family could have dreamed of in middle school. I found love, became the mother of four sons, and now enjoy the privilege of four daughters-in-love and a growing number of grandchildren.

Sadly, mine is not always the story of the children who might find themselves confused in our day. Rather than encourage them that the awkwardness of this season will grow into something very different in the next, we allow them to feel trapped in their *now*. Do we rip out summer flowers in early spring because they have not yet flowered? No, we wait, water, weed, and protect their growth. If we are willing to do this for plants, how much more for our children?

> For everything there is a season, a time for every activity under heaven. (Eccles. 3:1 NLT)

The awkwardness of adolescence should not be magnified into a problem to be fixed. It is a season of growth and change. The uncomfortable feelings associated with their changing bodies are exacerbated when children are sexualized rather than protected. The various avenues of social media have played the pied piper and led children away from their parents. And for what reason? Tragically, it's mostly for money. Nelson Mandela once said,

> The true character of a society is revealed in how it treats its children.[6]

Our children are experiencing a loss of innocence. Why are we allowing this?

Common Sense, Common Language

I've shared two of my recent conversations with my grand-daughters. I'm sure you've had some conversations of your own where what was once understood is now in question. We can recognize this struggle in our use of language. Each month we are confronted with how language should be collectively used—what words mean and who decides their meaning. Recently, I watched an interview in which a female doctor referred to expectant women as "pregnant people." When the interviewer challenged her terminology and volunteered the words *women* or *mothers* as more precise word choices, she became defensive and countered that her word choices were inclusive.[7]

Inclusion shouldn't outweigh accuracy. "Pregnant people" confuses the matter. A female doctor knows that only biological females become pregnant. I understand that women are people, but so are men, and men are never pregnant people. I understand it was an attempt to include biological females who gender identify as a male. But after carrying and giving birth to four children, I am not willing to share the unique privilege of pregnancy with men.

The degradation of words weakens our language, which in turn weakens our connections. Twisting the meaning of words bends the structure of language. When the meanings of words are compromised, our ability to understand and communicate is undermined. When there is a state of confusion, people do not know how to relate. Even children are confused in a world where mothers are not women.

I believe language has been weaponized by our enemy to divide, disorient, and silence us. A word or phrase that meant one thing in the past means something entirely different in our present. When this happens, people become hesitant. Afraid

THE FIGHT FOR FEMALE

of misspeaking, people become echo chambers. I just checked, and currently the count on gender pronouns is around fifty.[8] A constantly expanding array of subjective pronouns is very difficult to keep track of.

Confusion becomes king as words lose their meaning. Disconnections become the breeding ground for strife, tension, and misunderstanding.

In his book *1984*, George Orwell introduced a concept known as "doublespeak," the deliberate distortion of language to disguise, obscure, hide, or reverse words' actual meanings.[9] His example of doublespeak was "War is Peace, Freedom is Slavery, Ignorance is Strength."[10]

One of our equations might read, "Confusion is clarity, wrong is right, lies are my truth."

What is the reasoning behind flipping the language? The answer is summed up well in the quote, "He who controls the language controls the masses."[11]

Let's define *language* to understand how it could control the masses. Language is "a **systematic** means of communicating ideas or feelings by the use of conventionalized signs, sounds, gestures, or marks having understood meanings."[12]

The opposite of systematic is chaotic. By definition, language is based on shared understanding. The dragon is fluent in chaos, which is widespread misunderstanding and misinformation. There is a constant threat of a communication breakdown when word usage and gestures change. For example, waving is recognized as a gesture of acknowledgment and greeting. But what happens if suddenly it becomes a sign of hostility? What formerly communicated welcome is now a threat of aggression. If I don't know the meaning of a wave has changed, I would think I'm communicating one thing while everyone else thinks I am saying something very different.

Words are the building blocks of language. But when their meanings crumble, it creates breaches in our understanding and instability in our conversations. When words are distorted, we lose our connection with reality and history. Without these tethers we are set adrift in a sea of misunderstanding.

> People organize their brains with conversation.
>
> Jordan B. Peterson[13]

Can we really afford to have disorganized brains? I know I certainly can't! My husband and I are both verbal processors. Being able to share thoughts, fears, dreams, and ideas with someone who knows, loves, and wants to understand you is a gift. So much confusion is eliminated through our conversations.

In addition to being how we communicate, language is how we learn, share ideas, express emotions, make meaningful connections, problem-solve, share answers, ask for help, and make and break vows. When word meanings are corrupted, our thoughts follow. My mother used to chide me, "Garbage in, garbage out."

It was her way of saying whatever you deposit is what will be available for you to withdraw.

Last winter, I babysat one of my grandsons, and whenever we walked by the fireplace, I stretched out my hand and firmly said, "Hot!" Now whenever he sees me and a fireplace, he declares, "Hot!" Between us, there is a clear understanding of the word.

If some words have been weaponized, then other words can be used to heal. Language can create or destroy, just as words have the power to heal or wound. For these reasons alone, words are sacred.

In his essay "Politics and the English Language," George Orwell proposed that there is no swifter route to the corruption of thought than through the corruption of language.[14] His words echo the wisdom of Proverbs.

> Wisdom will save you from the ways of wicked men,
> from men whose **words are perverse**,

> who have left the straight paths
> > to **walk in dark ways,**
> who **delight in doing wrong**
> > and **rejoice in the perverseness of evil,**
> whose **paths are crooked**
> > and who are **devious in their ways.** (2:12–15 NIV,
> > > emphasis added)

Perversity of speech leads to shadowed ways and the celebration of perverse evil. How are words perverted? *Merriam-Webster* explains it as the process of corrupting, misdirecting, misusing, or misinterpreting.[15] This means a word's former sense is altered, changed, misused, or misdirected so that the word is misinterpreted. Perverted language begins an exodus from the paths of light. The prophet Isaiah warned,

> Woe to those who call evil good
> > and good evil,
> who put darkness for light
> > and light for darkness,
> who put bitter for sweet
> > and sweet for bitter! (5:20)

And here we are. Lust is called love. Men are called women. Women are pregnant people, chest feeders, and bleeders. Evil is called good and good is called evil. Rebellion is freedom, and anything that stands in the way of self-fulfillment is considered hate and bondage. In days of distorted words, the remedy is a return to God's Word.

The tower of Babel proved the impossible will become possible when people are united in language and purpose. Our adversary the dragon is not ignorant; he knows the construction of the unholy ancient tower of Babel was stopped when the people no longer understood one another. The project was abandoned, and the disobedient people were scattered when their common language was deconstructed (Gen. 11). In the same way, he hopes to undermine the construction of a holy temple, the body of Christ.

> [Jesus] in whom the whole structure, being joined together, grows into a holy temple in the Lord. In him you also are being built together into a dwelling place for God by the Spirit. (Eph. 2:21–22)

The Word of God is the language we speak and allow to direct the course of our lives. But when words are corrupted, the holy text is distorted. Jesus is the living Word, which is yet another reason why the perverting of words is so diabolical. In 1 Corinthians 14, Paul addresses the issue of confusion in the Corinthian church.

> There are doubtless many different languages in the world, and none is without meaning, but if I do not know the meaning of the language, I will be a foreigner to the speaker and the speaker a foreigner to me. (vv. 10–11)

Paul addressed the inability of people to understand the meaning of the words spoken in other languages (unknown tongues) at a believers' meeting. This same challenge presents itself when I minister in another country. Because I do not speak or understand their language, I work with an interpreter so that what I say in English is understood. But what if I said "husband" and they translated it "boyfriend"? I'd have no way of knowing what they said, and everyone else would be confused by the nonsense.

> **Nonsense**, noun: words or language having no meaning or conveying no intelligible ideas; language, conduct, or an idea that is absurd or contrary to good sense.[16]

Nonsense is noise without understanding. As part of his example, Paul says,

And if the bugle gives an indistinct sound, who will get ready for battle? (1 Cor. 14:8)

Sounds without meaning create more questions than answers. When surrounded by inarticulate or confusing sounds, people don't know how to respond. Was that a call to arms or the signal for retreat? When you know the meaning of what you hear, you have a way forward.

You may have heard, "Sometimes the easiest way to solve a problem is to stop participating in the problem." I agree. We can use precise language without being hateful. For example, I will never call myself a cis woman. I will never call a woman with child a pregnant person. I cannot control how others refer to me, but I will refer to myself according to my female biology. There is no reason to behave otherwise. I am a woman.

We've all been invited to participate in the corruption of language and the misuse of words. People want us to say things we don't mean or believe and use confused words without meaning. I was taught that these practices are at best flattery and at worst lying, and anything in the middle is nonsense. There comes a point when participation becomes validation.

When lying is thought a kindness and foolishness is considered wisdom, it is time for us to opt out of the conversation. In my eyes, it is the same thing as pretending a dragon is harmless by petting it.

Because we care, we cannot be careless with what we say and what we choose not to say. Let's protect words like *female* and *male, son* and *daughter, woman* and *man, brother* and *sister,* and *mother* and *father.* If words are eliminated from our language, it isn't long before they are lost to our world. The unheard becomes the unspoken, and the unspoken becomes the unseen.

Don't think that I am equating the unseen with the invisible; rather, think of it as something or someone unrecognizable.

The Power of Language

The words we speak to one another matter.

The words we say to ourselves matter.

The words others have spoken over us matter.

These are some of the many reasons we should choose our words wisely. Words are not merely a collection of letters. They are expressions of the soul. When we no longer say what we mean, we no longer mean what we say, and our heart breaks a little. Just as the misuse of words can trap and ensnare us, the correct words release us. In times of darkness, God's Word is our lamp.

> Your word is a lamp to my feet
> and a light to my path. (Ps. 119:105)

It is time to be fluent in the language of our making. Our heavenly Father has given us His Word so that when we don't know what to think, we can adopt His perspective.

> For my thoughts are not your thoughts,
> neither are your ways my ways, declares the LORD.
> For as the heavens are higher than the earth,
> so are my ways higher than your ways
> and my thoughts than your thoughts.
>
> For as the rain and the snow come down from heaven
> and do not return there but water the earth,
> making it bring forth and sprout,
> giving seed to the sower and bread to the eater,
> so shall my word be that goes out from my mouth;
> it shall not return to me empty,

but it shall accomplish that which I purpose,
and shall succeed in the thing for which I sent it.
(Isa. 55:8–11)

His Word is His will. His Word reveals His thoughts. His Word reveals His ways. May our words reflect His grace to this earth, blessing it with good rather than evil, refreshment rather than drought, and order rather than chaos. That His kingdom would come and His will would be done. May we choose our words wisely and create pathways forward.

———

What conversations trip you up the most?

What is one thing you can do to use language more clearly?

What is one thing you can pray about?

CHAPTER 11

The Cultural Fight for Female

When men stop believing in God, they don't believe in nothing;
they believe in anything.

G. K. Chesterton

I am a citizen of two nations.

The United States is the land of my birth, and Italy is the land of my heritage. I am fluent only in English, and yet Italy speaks a language we all understand—history. Nero was one of Rome's most notorious emperors. His first wife was Octavia; it was a marriage of political convenience. It wasn't long before he falsely accused her of adultery, and after her execution, he married his mistress, Sabina. This marriage ended poorly as well when Nero allegedly kicked Sabina to death in AD 65 (some accounts say while she was pregnant). Nero's third wife, and empress of Rome, was a sixteen-year-old male slave named Sporus, whom Nero had castrated and dressed as a woman.[1]

Does any of this sound in any way familiar? Corrupt politically motivated leaders? A disregard for marriage and life? We are in the process of witnessing our nation's cultural demise.

British author and journalist Douglas Murray made this point in a recent interview:

> The whole nonbinary thing is a brilliant one if you wanted to pull apart society because, again, [you] get people to pretend that men and women don't exist. . . . Say there's no difference between men and women. . . . If you do that stuff, then of course people end up, they just doubt everything, everything. And that's why these things worry some of us, because if everybody is persuaded to doubt what they see with their eyes, then they can be persuaded to fall for absolutely anything next.[2]

When people doubt everything, it opens the door to them believing anything. Every time I think the "anything goes" mindset cannot become more ridiculous or inane, it does. But I shouldn't be surprised because the Roman Empire proves that we have been here before.

> Those who cannot remember the past are condemned to repeat it.
>
> George Santayana[3]

I began this chapter with this quote by G. K. Chesterton: "When men stop believing in God, they don't believe in nothing; they believe in anything."

We cannot go along with culture and its belief in everything and anything. To believe in God is to believe what He says.

Biological women are experiencing an identity theft that threatens the truth of our divine origin. Recently women were gifted the prefix *cis* to designate women whose "assigned" biological sex and "gender identity" agreed. But the use of the term *assigned* is an attempt to undermine the fact that our DNA is divinely woven. It is God-given rather than arbitrarily assigned at birth. At the dawn of our creation, *woman* was the name gifted to us.

Genesis 2:19 tells the story of the man's God-given ability to name:

> And whatever the man called every living creature, that was its name.

Names are significant. They have the power to create associations between words and imagery. When we hear someone's name, we see the person. When God brought the woman to the man, he declared,

> This at last is bone of my bones
> and flesh of my flesh;
> she shall be called Woman,
> because she was taken out of Man. (v. 23)

This designation, "she shall be called Woman," leaves no provision for "he shall be called Woman." We were taken out of the man; he cannot wear us on the outside.

Woman is *our* creation name.

As such, any prefix dilutes or distorts our name, and we will not be "unnamed." The name *woman* is meant to be shared only among females. I adhere to the biblical belief that there are only two sexes—male and female—and the classical idea that these sexes have two corresponding genders—male and female—and that within each, there is freedom of expression.

> Woman is our creation name.

Prefixes unnecessarily undermine and confuse. The prefix *cis* means "on the same side of."[4] This was added to make way for the category of "trans." As a note of interest, the prefix *trans* means "on the other side of," "across," "beyond," or "to change or transfer."[5] The other side of woman will always be man. By definition, *trans* suggests that men and women can change sides. This is not God's perspective.

Please understand I have no desire to be cruel. I am not addressing intersex; I understand that intersex exists. This biological challenge occurs in 0.005–0.018 percent of births, where both male and female gonads are present.[6] This condition is physical and recognizable. Doctors work with their intersex patients to determine what is the most compatible sex/gender for them to adopt. This is the only case where assigning a sex/gender makes sense. Also, in no way do I want to minimize the agonizing struggle of those who truly suffer from gender identity disorder (which occurs in 2–3 females per 100,000 and 5–14 males per 100,000).[7]

What I want to address is how quickly biological sex has been pushed aside in favor of the idea that gender is merely a social construct rather than an expression aligned with our biological sex. Gender identity is not the same as intersex; it is how someone feels about their biological sex.

Basic examples of gender as a social construct are that girls wear pink and boys wear blue. Girls play with dolls; boys play with cars. But what if a girl wants to wear blue and play with cars? Or what if a boy wants to wear pink and play with dolls? I believe the answer to these questions is to allow for a spectrum of gender expressions in which girls can unashamedly be "tomboys" (my bent growing up) and boys can be nurturing.

This seems a much kinder option than saying that our children's sex and gender are misaligned and pursuing a protocol of lifelong hormone use and surgeries that are proving to compromise their long-term health and ability to reproduce.

My hope is to recover a sense of sanity and clarity. Growing up, I preferred the company of boys, but I never thought I was one. Looking back, my tomboy tendencies helped foster an understanding of males I'd one day need as a mother to four of them. And yet, is gender only a collection of behavioral patterns, personality traits, and preferences? There was a time when I never wanted to marry and another time when I was young that I wanted to be an astronaut. But I married, became a mother, and eventually became an author.

We cannot forget what it means to be a woman.

> Worse followed. Refusing to know God, they soon didn't know how to be human either—women didn't know how to be women, men didn't know how to be men. (Rom. 1:26 MSG)

We've lost our way when men and women forget their humanity and no longer remember how to connect with and care for one another.

To accommodate the plight of the truly gender dysphoric, women made the concession to allow a small percentage of men who dressed as women to share our bathrooms. But this allowance has morphed into an invasion of other spaces. Suddenly men with no previous history of gender dysphoria decided to self-identify as women. Our daughters have been physically and sexually assaulted in formerly safe spaces. Women have been raped by sex offenders who now identify as women in prisons. Girls have been assaulted in school hallways and bathrooms.[8] Perhaps you missed the video where a middle school boy, dressed as a girl, beat up a girl in the hallway of their school as their classmates watched. No one stepped in to help her . . . they were too busy recording the altercation on their phones.[9]

Here is my concern: biological women who have transitioned by way of hormones, surgery, or self-declaration to "trans men" are not a threat to the safety of men. I've yet to see or hear stories of trans men outpacing or injuring men in athletics or professional sports. Trans men do not sexually assault male inmates in prisons, and males are not afraid of sharing public bathrooms or school locker rooms with trans men. The safety of biological women is not threatened by trans men. But women are being threatened and attacked by "trans women" (biological men).

Even when women felt sexualized to the extreme, we remained civil and tolerant as drag queens left the confines of adult clubs and invaded our children's spaces of schools, libraries, and holiday celebrations. We were told to agree with the parodies of female. Girls who competed to be prom and homecoming queens stepped aside and let young men win.[10]

Trans women have been named "Woman of the Year."[11] And women the world over are largely silent, or strangely supportive. How can we be okay with this? Have we forgotten what it means to be a woman? People clap as biological women are stripped of titles that once solely belonged to women but are now awarded to a beautiful but sexualized version of womanhood. Two nations sent trans women as representatives for the Miss Universe pageant.[12] Is it right to support inclusion by excluding women? If this continues, what will our daughters inherit?

> You cannot love a thing without wanting to fight for it.
>
> G. K. Chesterton[13]

Our children are worth fighting for.

After I spoke at a recent women's event, a pastor's wife pulled me aside. She asked me if I had known a specific minister who had done missionary work all over the world but had passed away a while ago. I explained that I'd heard of him but never met him. She shared that she'd hosted a women's event decades earlier with him as the speaker. Afterward, they noticed he was weeping. Alarmed, they asked him what was troubling him. He shared, "I see an attack coming against the women, and if the enemy gets the women, he will get the children."

It is happening.

Our children are at risk, and the threat is both physical and emotional. In my hometown, a trans man (biological woman) shot three six-year-old children and three adults in their sixties at a Christian school.[14] Atrocities of this nature are rarely committed by a woman. Women tend to protect life rather than take it. But then again, I question any woman's ability to process the aggression that would come with doses of testosterone high enough to chemically change a woman into a man.

Some public school systems have shifted their educational programs to accommodate gender ideologies. Teachers who won't comply have been forced out of their positions.[15] Elementary age children known as sons or daughters in the sanctuary of their homes are encouraged to question their gender. *How do you know you're a boy? Are you sure you're still a girl?*

The youth and children's sections of our public and school libraries are flooded with illustrated pornographic literature that targets children.[16] Parents have been physically removed from school board meetings that they've attended to protest the inclusion of these materials. They have been removed for reading excerpts or showing illustrations from these books. Officials have found the material too offensive for a meeting attended by adults. But rather than remove the books, they have removed the parents.[17] This has caused a number of parents to pull their children out of public education, which is a thin layer of protection if their children have access to social media or if their children's friends do.

In recent years, the number of youths identifying as transgender has doubled.[18] Our medical establishments are encouraged not to question rapid-onset gender dysphoria but to affirm it and proceed with a medical protocol.

In some clinics, it has become the cure for all ills. Depressed? Perhaps you're the wrong gender. Unpopular? Have you considered changing your gender? Uncomfortable in your teenage body? Why not try cross hormones and a top surgery? The consequences of these choices can range from never having children to never nursing a child they might carry.

Chances are, some of you know someone who has been told these very things. They were told changing their gender would solve all their woes, and perhaps for a moment they felt it did. But then they realized their troubles were only compounded. The drastic changes they made to their body failed to fix the intimate brokenness in their soul. Perhaps you are a parent, or you know a parent, who has been told this is the only way forward for a struggling child with gender dysphoria.

People are hurting, and when people are in pain, they turn to whatever is put before them that promises relief. Desperate for answers, many go online to discuss their struggles with strangers rather than navigate their questions with family and close friends. Social media and online algorithms latch on to their plight and bombard them with messaging. Those desperate for hope are the most vulnerable to lies. There is a generation whose identity is assaulted each day. I must believe it is because the enemy knows if they ever discover their true identity . . . they will be a threat. I don't have all the answers, but I do know the One who is the truth. I believe as we move forward in consecrated prayer and constructive conversations, we will find answers along the way.

———

This chapter focused on exposing our cultural battle.

Did anything that I said upset you?

THE CULTURAL FIGHT FOR FEMALE

If so, what did you disagree with?

Were you aware of how far gender-identity confusion has reached?

How has your perspective changed on what it means to be a female?

Where have the cultural messages about identity shown up in your life?

What is one thing you can do to combat cultural lies? Can you talk to your children? Get involved in the school board? Start cultural conversation groups in your neighborhood?

CHAPTER 12

The Fight against Idols

Little children, keep yourselves from idols.

1 John 5:21

Decades ago, my husband, John, was responsible for hosting the ministers who came to speak at the church we attended. One missionary he hosted invited us to join him for an early breakfast. I was slightly afraid of this man. He came off like a gruff, grumpy old man. But at this breakfast, I discovered another side of him. He was a big teddy bear. We listened intently as he shared story after story of his years as a missionary overseas.

As our time together was coming to an end, the conversation took a turn. Rather than share what he'd seen in the past, he warned us of things to come. At the time we listened in disbelief. Sadly, what he shared that day painted the world we live in today. Later, when John and I were alone in our car, we both questioned something he'd said that neither of us understood. He

THE FIGHT FOR FEMALE

was adamant that a day was coming when people's lives would be controlled by a box they held in their hand.

How could a box control anyone? We wondered if he was having a senior moment. We couldn't imagine a box telling people what to do, let alone anyone listening to it. Boxes were for presents, packing, mailing, and storage. The year he shared this with us was 1984 or '85, back when phones lived on desks, nightstands, or walls.

Four decades later, this box thinks it's your boss. I'm not throwing anyone under the bus, but have you witnessed the panic people experience over a misplaced phone? I have seen this happen even when they are talking on it! If you are traveling, I get that. I'm referring to when they are home and were on their phone ten minutes earlier. The incessant demand of your phone will overwhelm you if you let it. Don't let it bully you.

And then there is the constant noise of social media that maximizes some voices and minimizes others. News outlets inundate our households with stories and images of violence, wanton crime, and theft. The news is a constant stream of negativity. Any sense of stability is shaken by threats of population control, food shortages, cancel culture, political corruption, wars, and rumors of wars. We were not created to take in hours of this much awful. Our homes should be havens.

The box listens carefully and utilizes algorithms to generate purchases and capture your attention with current interests. A constant array of curated distractions leads the unwary away from what matters. When parents have a phone in their hand, children feel as though they must compete for their attention. When children have a phone in their hand, parents have a hard time getting their attention. Husbands feel ignored by their wives and wives feel ignored by their husbands when the phone is present. It robs them of the time they have together.

Friends focused on capturing a photo of their time together can miss out on meaningful moments. We are not created to be

164

assailed by constant comparison or to live under the pressure to always present our lives to an audience of strangers. Life is more than a photo shoot, and your children and marriage are more than content for your social platform.

If you allow it to, the phone will constantly interrupt your life and conversations. Any guest who behaved this way would not be invited back. Even our children are trained not to interrupt because it is rude. And yet we let the phone behave in ways we'd never tolerate from others. Your phone is a tool. It is not your counselor or your intimate other. If the box in your hand undermines the life and relationships you want to build, put it back in the right place. When I turn my phone off at night, I say, "Good night, pretend world," and that is exactly what it is, a collection of pretenses.

> **If the box in your hand undermines the life and relationships you want to build, put it back in the right place.**

As potentially damaging as it is to our interpersonal relationships, it poses an even greater threat to our souls. Isaiah 30:15 tells us,

> For thus said the Lord God, the Holy One of Israel,
> "In returning and rest you shall be saved;
>   in quietness and in trust shall be your strength."
> But you were unwilling.

Rest is found when we turn from the idolatry of striving. When we choose to be still and know that He is the source of life and strength. When we trust that in chaos there is a clear path forward. Quiet can become uncomfortable when we've been conditioned to constant noise, but it is necessary. In the stillness we hear what the Spirit is saying, whether it is by way of meditating on the Scriptures, reading, prayer, a service, a song, or a friend.

Loud and constant noises have a way of desensitizing us from the quiet counsel of the Holy Spirit. When we put down the box, we can focus on aligning our heart with its Creator. Constant messaging could be likened to standing in front of a bass speaker whose loud vibrations compress your heart. And this type of heart compression has gone on for years. In times of loud, questioning chaos, the enemy makes a play for our worship.

What Do We Worship?

In the book of Daniel, this conflict played out in a dynamic way. King Nebuchadnezzar commanded all his subjects—which included the Israelites who were in Babylonian captivity—to bow before his golden image (an idol) whenever any form of music was played, whether it was a single instrument or a cacophony of sound.

> And the herald proclaimed aloud, "You are commanded, O peoples, nations, and languages, that when you hear the sound of the horn, pipe, lyre, trigon, harp, bagpipe, and every kind of music, you are to fall down and worship the golden image that King Nebuchadnezzar has set up. And whoever does not fall down and worship shall immediately be cast into a burning fiery furnace." (3:4–6)

It would seem the more ridiculous the command, the more severe the punishment. The king gave two choices: hit the ground or death by fire. Like Lucifer, Nebuchadnezzar understood that music had the power to make emotional connections. We remember what we sing, just as to a lesser degree we have memories attached to songs. This king claimed all the power of music and the sounds of *all* the musical instruments for the worship of his idol. Three Hebrew men refused. They worshiped their Hebrew God alone. Bowing would mean lifting their souls up to an idol, a practice their God strictly forbade. Outraged by their rebellion, the king sent for them and extended another chance for his wise counselors to bow down.

> "Is it true, O Shadrach, Meshach, and Abednego, that you do not serve my gods or worship the golden image that I have set up? Now if you are ready when you hear the sound of the horn, pipe, lyre, trigon, harp, bagpipe, and every kind of music, to fall down and worship the image that I have made, well and good. But if you do not worship, you shall immediately be cast into a burning fiery furnace. And who is the god who will deliver you out of my hands?" (vv. 14–15)

You will be given multiple opportunities to compromise. Don't do it. If you know you were right the first time, stick with it. I want to highlight a few thoughts in this passage. First, Nebuchadnezzar attached his identity to these gods and the image. This attachment is reflected in his words "my gods" and "worship the golden image that I have set up." Next, as aforementioned, the elaborate musical instruments and options were an attempt to dominate every other form of music and create a concert of chaos. And last, the king put himself on level with the Holy One of Israel by saying no god could rescue them out of his hand.

> **You will be given multiple opportunities to compromise. Don't do it.**

> Shadrach, Meshach, and Abednego answered and said to the king, "O Nebuchadnezzar, we have no need to answer you in this matter. If this be so, our God whom we serve is able to deliver us from the burning fiery furnace, and he will deliver us out of your hand, O king. But if not, be it known to you, O king, that we will not serve your gods or worship the golden image that you have set up." (vv. 16–18)

It's tempting to argue, *Where's the harm if you know it is not a god? Just bow. Indulge him. It's not worth losing your life.* I love their response: "We have no need to answer you in this matter." In other words, they are saying this isn't up for discussion; the issue is settled. This infuriated the king, and he ordered his men to raise the temperature sevenfold. It was so hot, the men who tossed Shadrach, Meshach, and Abednego into the furnace were killed by the heat.

> Shadrach, Meshach, and Abednego fell bound into the burning fiery furnace.
>
> Then King Nebuchadnezzar was astonished and rose up in haste. He declared to his counselors, "Did we not cast three men bound into the fire?" They answered and said to the king, "True, O king." He answered and said, "But I see four men unbound, walking in the midst of the fire, and they are not hurt; and the appearance of the fourth is like a son of the gods." (vv. 23–25)

The math didn't add up. Three men bound and dropped in does not equal four free and walking around.

> Then Nebuchadnezzar came near to the door of the burning fiery furnace; he declared, "Shadrach, Meshach, and Abednego, servants of the Most High God, come out, and come here!" Then Shadrach, Meshach, and Abednego came out from the fire. (v. 26)

They simply walked away from the flames.

> Nebuchadnezzar answered and said, "Blessed be the God of Shadrach, Meshach, and Abednego, who has sent his angel and delivered his servants, who trusted in him, and set aside the king's command, and yielded up their bodies rather than serve and worship any god except their own God." (v. 28)

It is one thing to sing about another in the fire—and quite another to live the reality of this. The king's words, "who trusted in him, and set aside the king's command, and yielded up their bodies rather than serve and worship any god except their own God," lend us insight on ways to avoid idolatry.

The time will come when trusting God will mean just such a choice will be put before you. Don't argue and don't bow. You can refuse to conform without being contentious. Our bodies are now temples reserved for the service and worship of God alone. In 2 Corinthians 6:16 Paul admonishes us,

> What agreement has the temple of God with idols? For we are the temple of the living God; as God said,
>
> > "I will make my dwelling among them and walk among them,
> > and I will be their God,
> > and they shall be my people."

God's temple has no agreement with or room for idols. We celebrate our bodies as God-given instruments of worship. Paul goes on to say,

> > "Therefore go out from their midst,
> > and be separate from them, says the Lord,
> > and touch no unclean thing;
> > then I will welcome you,
> > and I will be a father to you,
> > and you shall be sons and daughters to me,
> > says the Lord Almighty."
>
> Since we have these promises, beloved, let us cleanse ourselves from every defilement of body and spirit, bringing holiness to completion in the fear of God. (6:17–7:1)

Paul is citing the prophet Isaiah. We are separate in our worship and pursuit, but touching a pig or a lizard no longer makes us unclean. Our high priest Jesus made us righteous before God from the inside out. The defilement of idolatry is addressed when we embrace the fear of God.

In 1 John 5:21 we're admonished, "Little children, keep yourselves from idols." Then in 1 Corinthians 10:14, we are told, "Therefore, my beloved, flee from idolatry."

But how?

In their day, idols were housed in temples; in our day, the idols might be found in our houses! To recognize the influence of idols or an area of idolatry in our life, let's first define *idol*: "an object of extreme devotion; a representation or symbol of an object of worship; a false god; a likeness of something; a false conception; fallacy; a form or appearance visible but without substance."[1]

Idols deal in appearances rather than actualities. As such, idols will prove false to those who worship or trust in them. Idols belittle the greatness of the God Most High. Even though they demand that we bow down, they fail to raise us. Comparison is the common companion of the idol of self.

The Bible uses the words *idols*, *gods*, and *images* interchangeably. Idols are created when we turn to that which is less and treat it as more; as a source of identity instead of the God Most High. Idolatry is often the practice of engaging with the right things in a wrong way. For example, marriage, children, a career, friends, a spouse, food, sports, and even exercise are all good things, but if we attach too much importance to any of these, they can potentially become an idol. In my case, if I pursue ministry to the neglect of the health of my marriage or my personal relationship with my Savior, it has the wrong place in my life. Both Exodus 20:4 and Deuteronomy 5:8 carry God's warning:

You must not make for yourself an idol of any kind. (NLT)

We are the ones who empower or create idols by where we place our trust and affection. This happens when we give our strength to or draw our strength or comfort from sources outside our Creator. This could mean we have the wrong focus and are looking for the right thing in the wrong place or we've made ourselves the source. In keeping in line with this reasoning, addictions are a form of idolatry. Entertainment can become idolatry. Or maybe we trusted in a career to establish ourselves rather than trusting the One who empowers us to create wealth to establish His covenant.

> We are the ones who empower or create idols by where we place our trust and affection.

Colossians 3:5 tells us that covetousness is idolatry. Covetousness is desiring and wanting something more than God or His will for your life. Paul referenced the idolatry of the children of Israel as our example.

> Do not be idolaters as some of them were; as it is written, "The people sat down to eat and drink and rose up to play." We must not indulge in sexual immorality as some of them did, and twenty-three thousand fell in a single day. . . . **Now these things happened to them as an example, but they were written down for our instruction, on whom the end of the ages has come.** (1 Cor. 10:7–8, 11, emphasis added)

They had created a golden calf, then copied the worship practices of Egypt. Their idolatry involved unrestrained sexual and self-indulgence just as it does today. The hollow idol of self-indulgence enslaves its adherents to appetites that can never be satisfied. In the end, the insatiable desires isolate us from what and whom we love.

The Idol of Self

Our image—the way we think about ourselves and the image we project to others—can become an idol that promises us happiness and fulfillment. As Fyodor Dostoevsky wrote in *The Brothers Karamazov,*

> The world says: "You have needs—satisfy them. You have as much right as the rich and the mighty. Don't hesitate to satisfy your needs; indeed, expand your needs and demand more." This is the worldly doctrine of today. And they believe that this is freedom.[2]

This type of idolatry encourages us to live for ourselves—then hands us a mirror that reflects all that we lack. The image in this one-dimensional glass only confirms what we already feared: that we will never be enough. Not young enough, pretty enough, thin enough, feminine enough, influential enough, rich enough, loved enough, or successful enough. Any praise this idol might lend is temporary and quickly snatched away when someone who has or does *more* presents themselves.

The Idol of Religion

The idolatry of religion implies that you must make yourself good enough. Religion is a collection of impossible rules and formulas. At first a list of rules might appear easier than serving a living God who wants relationship. The religious mindset is rooted in pride and its cousin false humility. In forty years in ministry, I've witnessed so many who started out humble and ended up trapped in sin or works. But for me, the idol of religion is most obviously in play when one faction of the body of Christ or one religious denomination attacks another. Religious idolatry is mean-spirited. This idol builds platforms by tearing other people and religions down through its partnership with judgment.

Most women have experienced this distortion in one way or another. There are many variations of this. Women are welcome to come to church but not speak in church. Women can speak in church, but only if they are sharing. Women can speak, but not in an authoritarian way. Women can speak but not lead. You get the point. There are many variations and opinions, ranging from extreme complementarian to progressive egalitarian.

What I want to address is the way this mixed messaging implies that the death of Jesus was powerful enough to save and completely redeem men, but women are going to need to put in some work. Some denominations go as far as telling their women childbearing will save them. This only makes sense if we believe the redemption of women was only partially accomplished.

If we want to take Scripture literally, then women must stop talking from the moment they enter the building until the moment they exit.

Recently my team posted a clip of me speaking to a stadium of women. Several men posted verses from 1 Timothy about the silence of women in the church. The fact that I wasn't in a church didn't seem to matter. One man explained that if any clips of me speaking were posted where a man might see them, there would be a corruptive effect on the church. He further explained that women preaching was the highest form of spiritual evil. I wish I could tell you that I was making this up or that this type of rhetoric was an isolated incident, but I can't. Proving again that the idol of religion is unreasonable and will not be pleased.

The idol of religion tells us that we will never be godly enough, kind enough, biblical enough, or busy enough. And that's true, because if we could have been enough, God would not have sent His Son. Making ourselves "enough" has proven humanly impossible. Jesus alone is our salvation.

A cousin of the idol of religion is the idol of ministry. Under the sway of this idol, pastors or ministers become the focus rather than Jesus, our Savior. Ministry leaders have been known to neglect their marriages, families, and personal time with God in the pursuit of ministry. Pastors run the risk of thinking they play by different rules than the people they minister to. Which in one way is true; they play by stricter guidelines.

In the New Testament, Paul addresses idolatry as a work of the flesh.

> Now the works of the flesh are evident: sexual immorality, impurity, sensuality, idolatry, sorcery, enmity, strife, jealousy, fits of anger, rivalries, dissensions, divisions, envy, drunkenness, orgies, and things like these. I warn you, as I warned you before, that those who do such things will not inherit the kingdom of God. (Gal. 5:19–21)

Idols and works of the flesh are intertwined. Other versions of verse 21 say "those who practice such things." Something that we practice is something that has become a habit. Habits are practices we do without thinking.

Earlier in this book, I talked about my eating disorder—this was not only a breach between my body and spirit, but it became an idol that controlled me. When something gains a level of mastery over us that it shouldn't have, idolatry is involved. When I confessed that my weight and food were idols, I was set free. I've dealt with other forms of idolatry since then. And God is more than willing to address anything that holds His children captive.

The Snare of the Fear of Man

More recently, I have wrestled with possibly the most daunting idol I've encountered . . . the opinions of others. The fear of man looms large. There is so much pressure for us to bow to the ever-changing dictates of others—both those we know and those we don't.

This is not a new battle or a new ploy of the enemy. He has been wanting God's people to bow for quite some time. And this idol rarely comes alone—when we feel pressure to bow to opinion, almost always the idol of self is also present, urging us to think about our reputation, our image, or the fear of what might happen if we don't go along. We escape the fear of man by embracing the fear of God. It is not enough to simply acknowledge that there are immutable truths; our lives should agree with truth.

John addressed the believers of his day with this exhortation:

> We know that we are from God, and the whole world lies in the power of the evil one.
>
> And we know that the Son of God has come and has given us understanding, so that we may know him who is true; and we are in him who is true, in his Son Jesus Christ. He is the true God and eternal life. (1 John 5:19–20)

John clearly outlines here those who are within and those who are without. Those "in Christ" and those under the sway of the evil one. As those who are in Christ, we are called to a different life.

Free to Choose

> It is absolutely clear that God has called you to a free life. Just make sure that you don't use this freedom as an excuse to do whatever you want to do and destroy your freedom. Rather, use your freedom to serve one another in love. (Gal. 5:13 MSG)

Jesus calls us to lives of freedom. This gift of freedom grows as we reach out to others and shrinks when we live only for ourselves. Self-indulgence is a pathway to destruction. The emancipation of self is found in death to self and life in Christ. But freedom is a fragile thing; it must be tended. Liberty requires our thought, our will, and our trust in the One who gave it to us.

> There are two freedoms—the false, where a man is free to do what he likes; and the true, where a man is free to do what he ought.
>
> Charles Kingsley[3]

THE FIGHT FOR FEMALE

In light of this, freedom is the ability to do the right and possibly hardest thing (what one ought) rather than choose the wrong and often easier thing. Freedom is not the same as rebellion, and yet you are free to rebel even though you won't like where it brings you. Christ frees us to choose what is right, what is true, and what is just. You are free to live beyond yourself and aware of others. You are also free to be self-aware rather than self-absorbed.

Each day brings us choices. Who we speak with, how we speak with them, what we consume, and how we spend our time, talent, and resources are all choices. Some choices are momentary, and others are monumental, reaching into future generations.

> I have set before you life and death, blessing and curse. Therefore choose life, that you and your offspring may live, loving the LORD your God, obeying his voice and holding fast to him, for he is your life and length of days. (Deut. 30:19–20)

This passage highlights the incredible power of choice. Just as God set these choices before the children of Israel, He sets them before us. When we choose Christ, we choose life.

> Then Jesus told his disciples, "If anyone would come after me, let him deny himself and take up his cross and follow me." (Matt. 16:24)

Culture says believe in yourself; Jesus said believe in Me.

Culture says fulfill yourself; Jesus said deny yourself.

Culture says identify yourself; Jesus called you by name.

Culture says live for the moment; Jesus said this life is a vapor.

Culture says think obsessively of yourself; Jesus said think of others.

Culture says care only for yourself; our Lord said care for others.

Culture says blame others; Jesus said forgive and cancel their debt.

Culture says make excuses; Jesus said take responsibility.

Culture says conform; our Lord invites us to be transformed.

Christ is formed in us by our willing acts of obedience.

———

Which one of these commands from culture could you exchange with Jesus's command today?

What is one thing you can stop doing?

What is one thing you can pray?

CHAPTER 13

The Fight for Female Heroes

The best way to explain it is to do it.
Lewis Carroll,
Alice in Wonderland

Doesn't it feel as though we've fallen into Alice's upside-down world? Who hasn't been led down a few rabbit holes that required eating cake and drinking potions that made us too large or too small? We've cried, lost keys, conversed with confused strangers, and shared tea with some unusual characters. We've become embroiled in games without rules, and whenever we trip over a new word or violate an unknown ordinance, the cancel queen threatens to take off our heads. As confusing or frightening as all this might be, please recognize this collection of distractions as smoke screens designed to keep us from addressing our real enemy.

Alice's Wonderland had a dragon of its own, the Queen's Jabberwocky. In accordance with the annals of Wonderland, Alice was destined to slay this terrifying fiend, armed with the legendary Vorpal sword. In the 2010 movie *Alice in Wonderland*, the dragon and Alice exchange words before the battle commences. The dragon challenges, "So, my old foe, we meet on the battlefield once again."

Confused, Alice counters, "We have never met."

"Not you, insignificant bearer; my ancient enemy, the Vorpal one."[1]

In the same way, we are insignificant but what we carry is not. The dragon we face hates but does not fear us. He fears our King and recognizes His mark upon our life. He shudders at the sound of His name. The sword we bear is spoken rather than raised. The dragon fears the weight, not the volume, of our words. As we speak God's Word, it becomes an invincible, invisible, eternal sword of the Spirit. When we lift our voices in prayer, the dragon hears the thundering voice of the One who is the Word.

> God is strong, and he wants you strong. So take everything the Master has set out for you, well-made weapons of the best materials. And put them to use so you will be able to stand up to everything the Devil throws your way. (Eph. 6:10–11 MSG)

There is a quote about men I have heard a lot lately.

> Hard times create strong men, strong men create good times, good times create weak men, and weak men create hard times.
>
> G. Michael Hopf[2]

The question I want to ask is, What might strong women create?

Strong is not wrong.

If it was, God would not have gone to such lengths to provide us with such extensive and effective weaponry. And we are going to need them. Ephesians 6:12 tells us,

> This is no weekend war that we'll walk away from and forget about in a couple of hours. This is for keeps, a life-or-death fight to the finish against the Devil and all his angels. (MSG)

It is important to remember that words spoken but not obeyed are powerless. The Word of God is activated in our lives by belief and obedience. For too long, we've heard much and done little. The sword of the Spirit gains expression and power in our lives as we are doers of the Word rather than hearers only. When we uphold, believe, live, and obey, the Word of God gains full course in our lives, the enemy is held at bay. God will watch over His Word in our mouth and give us His words to speak.

In Christ, women are empowered individually and collectively. Jesus is the One who makes us a force for good. We are in a world that is hostile to women because it is hostile to life. A world that assigns more value to an employee or employer than to a mother. A world where marriage is maligned and children are seen as obstacles to careers and financial burdens. A world where men and women should be allies rather than competitors or even enemies. An upside-down world where women listen to the counsel of dragons and do not protect their children. And yet we have this promise. John 16:33 tells us,

> I have said these things to you, that in me you may have peace. In the world you will have tribulation. But take heart; I have overcome the world.

In Christ, we are in the world but not of it. We can dare to be encouraged. Dare to believe what we do can make a difference. Dare to believe the daughters of the Most High will rouse themselves and fight for female. We are here to oppose the brooding darkness with the light we bear. Even if we lose our lives, we win because we gain life eternal. We can't lose for His winning. But the dragon's destiny of defeat looms large before him and intends to do as much damage as possible in his allotted time. Revelation 12:12 punctuates our moment for us.

> But woe to you, O earth and sea, for the devil has come down to you in great wrath, because he knows that his time is short!

The fallen one, who led a third of the angels astray, fears the One who won the victory once and for all on the cross. With His death, Jesus "disarmed the spiritual rulers and authorities. He shamed them publicly by his victory over them on the cross" (Col. 2:15 NLT).

And as the darkness around us increases, it is easy to wonder, *Is something amiss? Is the enemy still armed?* The answer is yes and no. He was disarmed but not destroyed, displaced but not made captive. He was removed from heaven and moved to earth. His end draws near but is not yet realized. First Corinthians 15:24–26 tells us,

> Then comes the end, when he [Jesus] delivers the kingdom to God the Father after destroying every rule and every authority and power. For he must reign until he has put all his enemies under his feet. The last enemy to be destroyed is death.

The shadow of death is still a reality. It has yet to be swallowed up in Christ's victory. In John 5:24, Jesus gave us this promise:

> Truly, truly, I say to you, whoever hears my word and believes him who sent me has eternal life. He does not come into judgment, but has passed from death to life.

We no longer need to wrestle the specter of death and struggle to save ourselves. In Christ we have passed from death unto life and are empowered to leave behind selfishness and a self-absorbed mindset. We can follow the example of Jesus and the realization that there is no greater weapon than a life laid down. The words of Paul are as true today as when he admonished the first-century believers to live as children of light.

> With the Lord's authority I say this: Live no longer as the Gentiles do, for they are hopelessly confused. Their minds are full of darkness; they wander far from the life God gives because they have closed their minds and hardened their hearts against him. They have no sense of shame. They live for lustful pleasure and eagerly practice every kind of impurity. (Eph. 4:17–19 NLT)

I pray that the eyes of our understanding will be enlightened even as our minds are renewed. The English Standard Version of Ephesians 4:19 reads,

> They have become callous and have given themselves up to sensuality, greedy to practice every kind of impurity.

We have gone from *incidents* of impurity to the *practice* of every kind of impurity. We are the ones who choose what we will give ourselves to. Our choices are revealed in what we practice, and that is reflected by what we give our attention and affection to. Shame is not always an enemy. It can be an indication that you've done or said something shameful. It is a sign of health that means your heart is yet tender. We want to avoid the unhealthy pattern of making excuses. Life has taught me that once I own my mistakes, they no longer own me. We've all been through hard stuff and sinned and made some awful choices. Rather than justify those failures, let's lay them at the cross. Later in the book of Ephesians, Paul admonished the believers,

Let no one deceive you with empty words, for because of these things the wrath of God comes upon the sons of disobedience. Therefore do not become partners with them; for at one time you were darkness, but now you are light in the Lord. Walk as children of light. (5:6–8)

May each of us walk in the light of obedience. We are redeemed from the domination of sin to live under the dominion of Christ. Just as we are nothing without Him, we have access to everything we might need for life and godliness in Him. The enemy loves to capitalize on any ignorance we may have of who we are in Christ. He is the one who . . .

Tempts, then accuses, because he is the accuser.

Seduces, then shames.

Sexualizes in an attempt to rob us of our virtue.

Distorts the interpretation of Scripture to silence our voice.

The body of Christ needs to fight for female. The earth needs the voice of the sons and the daughters. Jesus has given us His authority, and the enemy has lost his authority.

Jesus came and said to them, "All authority in heaven and on earth has been given to me." (Matt. 28:18)

Jesus won more by His obedience than Adam and Eve forfeited through their disobedience. They had dominion on earth; Jesus won dominion over every realm. And what is the purpose of all this authority?

Go therefore and make disciples of all nations, baptizing them in the name of the Father and of the Son and of the Holy Spirit, teaching them to observe all that I have commanded you. And behold, I am with you always, to the end of the age. (Matt. 28:19–20)

And yet, I fear we've been content to simply go to church.

I believe we are at the end of an age. When you are given authority, you are authorized to use it. A day will come when we stand before the ultimate Authority and answer what we did with what His life purchased. Did we rescue others or enrich ourselves? The promise spoken to His disciples then is true of His disciples now. If someone placed a literal sword of light in your hand and told you that when that sword was lifted up, it had the power to heal, transform, liberate, save, impart wisdom, and empower those who carried it, would you put it in a closet? Or would you honor the entrustment and lift the sword high for all to see? We hold just such a weapon of light. The Word is alive, and its radiance overshadows our human inadequacies. Just like with Alice, the enemy sees what we bear, not what or who we've been.

Battles Reveal Heroes

> The godly people in the land
> are my true heroes!
> I take pleasure in them! (Ps. 16:3 NLT)

We learn by doing. Heroes are born in battles. Hard seasons reveal where we place our trust and garner our strength. Too many want to be heroes without fighting a battle. Heroes are made one choice at a time, one battle at a time. And godliness is created in us the same way—one God-honoring choice at a time.

History is punctuated with moments when the battle lines are clearly drawn. We find one of these as the book of Exodus opens. Two godly females commit the first recorded act of civil disobedience in Scripture to rescue male babies.

> Then the king of Egypt said to the Hebrew midwives, one of whom was named Shiphrah and the other Puah, "When you serve as midwife to the Hebrew women and see them on the birthstool,

if it is a son, you shall kill him, but if it is a daughter, she shall live." (1:15–16)

This king attempted an alliance of death with two women who were skilled in the practice of bringing life. He ordered the death of the Hebrew sons and allowed the daughters to live because he was afraid the Hebrews were growing too numerous and strong.

But the midwives feared God and did not do as the king of Egypt commanded them, but let the male children live. (v. 17)

I want to make the point that these women had no scriptural reference for their choice. And yet somehow, they equated honoring life with honoring God and refused the king. Some scholars say it is inconclusive whether these women were Egyptian or Hebrew. This question was raised due to their use of *Elohim* rather than *Yahweh*, and the fact that it would be unlikely that Pharaoh would have told Hebrew women to kill their own children.[3]

Time passed and the midwives' disobedience became obvious.

So the king of Egypt called the midwives and said to them, "Why have you done this, and let the male children live?" (v. 18)

Here is how they accounted for their choices:

The midwives said to Pharaoh, "Because the Hebrew women are not like the Egyptian women, for they are vigorous and give birth before the midwife comes to them." (v. 19)

I doubt this was completely true. They may have arrived late for some births, but surely not for all the Hebrew boys who were born.

So God dealt well with the midwives. And the people multiplied and grew very strong. And because the midwives feared God, he gave them families. (vv. 20–21)

God blessed the midwives with legacies of their own. There is no greater treasure in life than a legacy of godliness. When his plot with the midwives failed, the king made a bolder move and commanded *all* the Egyptians to murder the Hebrew males.

> Then Pharaoh commanded **all his people**, "Every son that is born to the Hebrews you shall cast into the Nile, but you shall let every daughter live." (v. 22, emphasis added)

Imagine the grief and horror these parents experienced. I wonder if neighbors reported one another. It's hard to understand the type of cruelty and hardness of heart involved in throwing infants into the Nile and watching from the shore as they drowned. And yet, far more infants in the US die each year by abortion than were drowned in Egypt. In our nation, there are women who take the lives of their children rather than rescue them. This leaves both our sons and daughters at risk. Culture has shifted, and Christians are increasingly considered a threat. We have the power to make courageous choices. As culture becomes progressively more godless, godliness will be at odds with worldly cultural directives.

The choice of one mother made way for the deliverance of a nation.

Amid the gendercide of Hebrew males in Egypt, one mother defied the king's decree and hid her son. I pray the tide will turn and we will see the same now.

> The woman conceived and bore a son, and when she saw that he was a fine child, she hid him three months. (Exod. 2:2)

She saw something special on her son. An angel hadn't appeared, and a prophet hadn't said, "I have a plan for this one." She simply saw and did.

Her courageous choice set something in motion. In a climate of chaos and death, she believed her son was worth the risk of defying her culture. She protected, nurtured, nursed, and I imagine wept over her son, knowing it was but a matter of time before she'd have to give him up. For three months a Hebrew family lived with a secret and hid an unnamed son. Ninety days is not very long.

> When she could hide him no longer, she took for him a basket made of bulrushes and daubed it with bitumen and pitch. She put the child in it and placed it among the reeds by the river bank. (v. 3)

She fashioned an ark for her child and prayed her son would be safe until he was rescued from the river where other sons had only found death. In the same way, our prayers weave an ark for our children that carries them when they leave our care. She chose the place among the reeds carefully and posted his sister to watch over him.

> And his sister stood at a distance to know what would be done to him. Now the daughter of Pharaoh came down to bathe at the river, while her young women walked beside the river. She saw the basket among the reeds and sent her servant woman, and she took it. (vv. 4–5)

Another woman saw and saved him. I don't believe this was an accidental encounter. The place Pharaoh's daughter bathed would have been specific. The Egyptians believed the Nile River was a sacred gateway to both life and death. Therefore, whatever the river brought to them was a gift from their gods.

> When she opened it, she saw the child, and behold, the baby was crying. She took pity on him and said, "This is one of the Hebrews' children." (v. 6)

An influential princess's heart was moved with compassion by the cry of a beautiful Hebrew child. She rescued the child, named him, and later adopted him as her own. "The princess named him Moses, for she explained, 'I lifted him out of the water'" (v. 10 NLT).

Miriam stepped forward and removed any barriers to Moses's rescue.

> Then his sister said to Pharaoh's daughter, "Shall I go and call you a nurse from the Hebrew women to nurse the child for you?" And Pharaoh's daughter said to her, "Go." So the girl went and called the child's mother. And Pharaoh's daughter said to her, "Take this child away and nurse him for me, and I will give you your wages." So the woman took the child and nursed him. (vv. 7–9)

Imagine their joy. The family was reunited, and now there was no more reason to fear for the life of Moses. He was protected by the royal family and his mother was employed by the pharaoh's daughter.

The first two chapters of Exodus are filled with female heroes. *Exodus* refers to freedom from Egypt and its way of life. Is God again positioning women to save, hide, protect, nurture, and provide for the next generation of heroes? Are we being set up for another exodus—a massive spiritual departure from false idols and ideologies—to return to true worship? If so, what part might we play? To answer, let's look again at what these women did in light of the quote that opened this chapter, "The best way to explain it is to do it."

God anoints skillful females.

The two midwives chose to practice godliness within their profession. They didn't have to leave their skill set to save lives. I believe the actions of these women had a catalytic effect that began the deliverance of the Hebrew nation. It's possible that Aaron, Moses's older brother, was born because of their choices. Their defiance might have emboldened Moses's mother. There is no way to know this for certain. Courage begets courage just as surely as cowardice begets cowardice. Thousands of years have passed, yet I am inspired by their bravery.

They are part of our story just as surely as we are part of theirs. My sisters, if you're a doctor, honor your vow to do no harm. If you're a teacher, educate the children entrusted to you. If you have any type of civil authority, use your position to protect and rescue. If you are part of the judicial system, fight for justice and truth. If you're a mother, protect and train your children in godliness.

God anoints females who see.

Moses's mother, Jochebed, saw something on her son. We need women who see the extraordinary within the ordinary. Women who see what others miss. Daughters who perceive the divine on and within their children, sisters, brothers, husbands, and friends. Women who disciple others in the fear of the Lord and the love of God. Women with mothers' hearts who see something good and godly on the generations that follow them. Women who nurture others with the milk of God's Word and release them into their next season once weaned.

Is there someone you see who needs protection, nurture, or preparation in this fight for female?

God anoints females who make connections.

Miriam was prophetically anointed to make timely and useful connections. She watched and waited until the princess found Moses. She connected the princess with someone who could provide nourishment for Moses. She connected a son at risk with a royal protector. Miriam grew into a prophetess and led the daughters of Israel in dance and joined her brother Moses in the first recorded song of worship (Exod. 15). We need women who make divine connections for provision and protection. Prophetic women who will war through worship and obedience. Dance that is divinely woven into worship is a weapon.

> We need women who see what others miss.

What connections for provision can you make?

Is there a song you need to write, sing, or dance to over your situation?

God anoints females with influence.

Pharaoh's daughter used her influence to rescue a life her kingly father had condemned. She was an advocate who used her position to lift the helpless. Any measure of influence we've been given is for God's glory. Her empathy was an integral part of Israel's deliverance. Her generosity provided Moses with an education and a home.

> Those of us who are strong and able in the faith need to step in and lend a hand to those who falter, and not just do what is most convenient for us. **Strength is for service, not status.** (Rom. 15:1 MSG, emphasis added)

This world needs women who are strong and able in faith rather than women who are weak and steeped in their fears. Angry women slap while faithful women lend a hand.

Service requires far more strength than status. Of course, service isn't seen or celebrated by people in the same ways status is, at least not now. But it will be rewarded by your Father in heaven. He faithfully rewards the very things others miss. If you secretly help someone who is struggling, it will carry a greater reward than posting your good deed on social media.

People are faltering all around us, and when people falter for a while, it is not long before they fall. The weight of discouragement and the stress of anxiety are at all-time highs. When someone falls, it is obvious that they need help, but faltering is easy to miss if we are not watching for it. This world will always pursue status over service. That is the very reason we cannot. We need women of unshakable, capable faith. Let's be women willing to

We need women of unshakable, capable faith.

step in and *do what needs to be done*, even when we are not seen or asked. Women who see the needs of those who falter and lend a hand. We need one another now more than ever. Daughters and sons need their mothers to be mothers. Husbands need their wives to be loving, wise, and capable. Sisters are in need of strong female friendships.

In the dream I shared in chapter 1, women carried and coddled the baby dragons. I can't help but think those dragons might represent the spiritual forces behind the ideologies that twist male and female. There were no men in the room I entered, only women. If they had only known, they would have broken the dragons' necks themselves and taken up swords to help their sisters do the same.

If the enemy would have presented itself in its truest form, the women would have cast away what they cradled. If they had understood that their kindness and care would not be reciprocated but mocked in the cruelest of ways. If they could have but discerned that the dragons' passion was not love or the desire to protect them; it was the patient hate of an ancient enemy that is willing to wait for the right moment to kill their children and waylay them with unbearable grief. So how do we win?

We Fight by Flourishing

"And you shall love the Lord your God with all your heart and with all your soul and with all your mind and with all your strength." The second is this: "You shall love your neighbor as yourself." There is no other commandment greater than these. (Mark 12:30–31)

When we find ourselves engaged in a war with a dragon, it is a mistake to fight fire with fire. He is the original accuser. Accusations only beget more accusations. These in turn grant the dragon an endless supply of flames. We will need a more powerful eternal element. We must dig deeper and fight by flourishing. In Isaiah 27, we see two parallel events: a revelation of God's judgment and the appearance of God's garden. Isaiah 27:1 opens with a prophetic window into the war between God and the dragon. It captures the redemption of both the true and the wild vine.

> At that time GOD will unsheathe his sword,
>> his merciless, massive, mighty sword.
> He'll punish the serpent Leviathan as it flees,
>> the serpent Leviathan thrashing in flight.
> He'll kill that old dragon
>> that lives in the sea. (MSG)

Even as this dragon meets his death, the vineyard comes to life. We see this glorious contrast in Isaiah 27:2–3:

> At that same time, a fine vineyard will appear.
>> There's something to sing about!
> I, GOD, tend it.
>> I keep it well-watered.
> I keep careful watch over it
>> so that no one can damage it. (MSG)

This is where we find ourselves in the story of the fight for female. We fight by bearing fruit from our connection with Jesus, our Vine. John 15 tells us that Jesus is our Vine and we, Jew and gentile, are His branches. Isaiah 27:4–5 goes on,

> I'm not angry. I care.
>> Even if it gives me thistles and thornbushes,
> I'll just pull them out
>> and burn them up.
> Let that vine cling to me for safety,
>> let it find a good and whole life with me,
>> let it hold on for a good and whole life. (MSG)

Isn't this beautiful?

By clinging to Him, we discover a good and whole life.

We flourish whenever we choose love.

Love is more than a feeling. Love is an action.

Love is a commandment that is always a choice.

I don't always get to choose how I feel, but I do get to choose how I respond. There are times when life demands acts of love when we are not experiencing the emotions or feelings of love. An exhausted mother will get up in the middle of the night to comfort a frightened or sick child because she is committed to loving her child. Love is a commitment. Love is our fail-safe because love cannot fail. Love never lies because it rejoices with truth.

Love requires courage, while hatred merely requires cowardice. The dragon hates love.

We have each been entrusted with something to love others with. If you are still wondering what that is, perhaps it is simply the thing you now have strength in but haven't known how to serve others with. Pause, press in, and ask the Holy Spirit what your gift is. It might be a skill, a gift of insight, a strategy, the ability to resource, to educate, to excel in business, or even something as selfless as providing a home for someone. The dragon fears females who have learned that you don't fight fire with fire; you fight fire with love.

May this be said of us. Let our lives tell the eternal story of mercy, in which male and female find their healing in Him. Let us live as Paul exhorts us in Philippians:

> Live clean, innocent lives as children of God, shining like bright lights in a world full of crooked and perverse people. (2:15 NLT)

Let's testify of the One who showed us the kindness that opened our ears to hear truth and whose mercy empowered us to turn from sin, shame, and blame. Rather than rehearse our narratives of rejection, let's speak of His ultimate adoption, available to all. Let's be brave enough to believe we are truly daughters of a divine kingdom, female ambassadors anointed by their Father to speak hope and healing.

Rather than highlight the friend who wasn't there for us, let's be the friend who is there for others. In so doing, we honor the One who promised never to leave us. Let's learn again the ways of our Prince of Peace, who was unjustly killed for our sins. In earthly wars people die, but we war for a kingdom of love where the dead are raised to new life.

> Rather than rehearse our narratives of rejection, let's speak of His ultimate adoption.

Women—let us prophesy His kingdom as we pursue lives of faith, hope, and love. May we remember the divine entrustment of female so that our Father, the God Most High, is glorified in our female form.

ACKNOWLEDGMENTS

The Fight for Female has easily been the most difficult book I have ever written. Therefore, I would be remiss if I didn't acknowledge my editor Andrea, whose patient wisdom has guided me throughout the painful process.

I want to thank my family and team, who sacrificed so much of their time with me as I trudged through this process. I love you all more than words.

NOTES

Chapter 1 Dreams, Dragons, and Daughters

1. Neil Gaiman, *Coraline* (New York: HarperCollins, 2002), epigraph. According to Gaiman, this is his paraphrase of a longer quote from G. K. Chesterton's book *Tremendous Trifles*. See https://neil-gaiman.tumblr.com/post/4290 9304300/my-moms-a-librarian-and-planning-to-put-literary.

2. Joseph Pearce, "Rescuing Our Maidens from the Culture of Death," The Imaginative Conservative, April 24, 2023 (orig. pub. Feb. 2016), https://the imaginativeconservative.org/2023/04/rescuing-maidens-culture-death-joseph -pearce.html.

3. Sara Jahnke, Nicholas Blagden, and Laura Hill, "Pedophile, Child Lover, or Minor-Attracted Person? Attitudes toward Labels among People Who Are Sexually Attracted to Children," *Archives of Sexual Behavior* 51, no. 8 (2022): 4125–4139, https://doi.org/10.1007/s10508-022-02331-6.

Chapter 3 The Fight for Your Sacred Space

1. Dr. Andrew Newberg and Mark Robert Waldman, *Words Can Change Your Brain* (New York: Avery, 2013), 3.

2. Abigail Shrier, *Irreversible Damage: The Transgender Craze Seducing Our Daughters* (Washington, DC: Regnery, 2020), 212.

3. N. T. Wright, *Paul for Everyone: Romans, Part 2: Chapters 9–16* (London: Society for Promoting Christian Knowledge, 2004), 70.

4. C. S. Lewis, *A Preface to Paradise Lost* (New York: HarperOne, 2022), 120.

5. Nancy R. Pearcey, *Love Thy Body: Answering Hard Questions about Life and Sexuality* (Grand Rapids: Baker Books, 2018), 223.

Chapter 4 The Fight in the Spirit Realm

1. N. T. Wright, *Paul for Everyone: The Prison Letters: Ephesians, Philippians, Colossians, and Philemon* (London: Society for Promoting Christian Knowledge, 2004), 72.

Chapter 5 The Fight for Generations

1. "'Dramatic' Decline in Worldwide Total Fertility Rates Predicted," Focus on Reproduction, July 23, 2020, https://www.focusonreproduction.eu/article /News-in-Reproduction-Population.

2. Prarthana Prakash, "Millennials and Gen Z Won't Have Enough Kids to Sustain America's Population—and It's Up to Immigrants to Make Up the Baby Shortfall," *Fortune*, January 25, 2023, https://fortune.com/2023 /01/25/us-population-growth-immigration-millennials-gen-z-deficit-births -marriage/.

3. "Mother Teresa Takes Pro-Life Message to the Supreme Court," EWTN Global Catholic Network, accessed December 21, 2023, https://www.ewtn .com/catholicism/library/mother-teresa-takes-prolife-message-to-the-supreme -court-2701. This article is taken from the February 24, 1994, issue of *The Arlington Catholic Herald*.

4. "Global and Regional Estimates of Unintended Pregnancy and Abortion," Guttmacher Institute, March 2022, https://www.guttmacher.org/fact -sheet/induced-abortion-worldwide. This statistic is also available from the World Health Organization, https://www.who.int/news-room/fact-sheets /detail/abortion.

5. Mona Lilja, Mikael Baaz, and Filip Strandberg Hassellind, "(Re)sketching the Theorizing around 'Missing Women': Imageries of the Future, Resistance, and Materializing Aspects of Gender," *International Feminist Journal of Politics* 25, no. 2 (2023): 266–87, https://doi.org/10.1080/14616742.2021.1981769.

6. Richard Fry, "A Record-High Share of 40-Year-Olds in the U.S. Have Never Been Married," Pew Research Center, June 28, 2023, https://www.pew research.org/short-reads/2023/06/28/a-record-high-share-of-40-year-olds -in-the-us-have-never-been-married/.

7. "Sexual Revolution: Definition, Liberation & Consequences," Study.com, updated November 21, 2023, https://study.com/learn/lesson/sexual-liberation -movement-origin-timeline-impact-revolution.html#:~:text=The%20sexual %20revolution%20was%20brought,Riots%2C%20and%20the%20Wood stock%20festival.

8. G. P. Joffe et al., "Multiple Partners and Partner Choice as Risk Factors for Sexually Transmitted Disease among Female College Students," *Sexually Transmitted Diseases* 19, no. 5 (1992): 272–8, https://doi:10.1097/00007435-1 99209000-00006.

9. "Global HIV & AIDS Statistics—Fact Sheet," UNAIDS, updated 2023, https://www.unaids.org/en/resources/fact-sheet.

10. Luke Gilkerson, "Get the Latest Pornography Statistics," Covenant Eyes, updated September 8, 2021, https://www.covenanteyes.com/2013/02 /19/pornography-statistics/; "Internet Pornography by the Numbers; A Significant Threat to Society," Webroot, accessed December 1, 2023, https:// www.webroot.com/us/en/resources/tips-articles/internet-pornography-by -the-numbers.

11. Jahnke, Blagden, and Hill, "Pedophile, Child Lover, or Minor-Attracted Person?"

12. Anjali Thakur, ed., "US Professor Stirs Controversy for Encouraging People to Read about Sex with Animals," NDTV World, updated November 13, 2023, https://www.ndtv.com/world-news/us-professor-stirs-controversy-for-encouraging-people-to-read-about-sex-with-animals-4570842.

13. Chrissy Sexton, "Lab-Grown Babies Could Become a Reality within Five Years," Earth.com, May 25, 2023, https://www.earth.com/news/lab-grown-babies-revolutionary-science-or-ethical-disaster/.

14. Aldous Huxley, *Brave New World* (London, 1932; Project Gutenberg Canada, 2016), chap. 3, https://gutenberg.ca/ebooks/huxleya-bravenewworld/huxleya-bravenewworld-00-h.html.

Chapter 6 The Fight for Lost and Found

1. Rav Chaim Navon, "The Woman in Creation," trans. David Strauss, Israel Koschitzky Torat Har Etzion, July 2, 2016, https://www.etzion.org.il/en/philosophy/issues-jewish-thought/topical-issues-thought/woman-creation.

Chapter 7 The Fight for Divine Alignment

1. Mallory Millett, "Marxist Feminism's Ruined Lives," *FrontPage Magazine*, September 1, 2014, https://www.frontpagemag.com/marxist-feminisms-ruined-lives-mallory-millett/.

2. Wikipedia, s.v. "Kate Millett," last modified February 8, 2024, https://en.wikipedia.org/wiki/Kate_Millett#:~:text=Millett%20came%20out%20as%20a,was%20married%20to%20Sophie%20Keir.

3. Robin Morgan, *Sisterhood Is Powerful: An Anthology of Writings from the Women's Liberation Movement* (New York: Vintage Books, 1970), 602.

4. Carolyn Susman, "Steinem Reminisces about Late Husband, Envisions Her Future," *The Ledger*, March 27, 2004, https://www.theledger.com/story/news/2004/03/27/steinem-reminisces-about-late-husband-envisions-her-future/26106870007/#:~:text=Steinem%2C%20the%20activist%20who%20had,animal%20rights%20activist%20David%20Bale.

5. See Jason Pierce, "Betty Friedan and the Women's Movement," Bill of Rights Institute, accessed March 28, 2024, https://billofrightsinstitute.org/essays/betty-friedan-and-the-womens-movement.

6. *Merriam-Webster*, s.v. "patriarch (n.)," accessed January 22, 2024, https://www.merriam-webster.com/dictionary/patriarch.

7. "So Babygirl! It's the New Gen Z Term of Endearment—But What Does It Mean?," The Guardian, January 24, 2024, https://www.theguardian.com/lifeandstyle/2024/jan/24/so-babygirl-its-the-new-gen-z-term-of-endearment-but-what-does-it-mean#:~:text=There%20is%20a%20conventional%20usage,the%20South%20Korean%20superstar%20Jimin.

8. Idil Karsit, "Why Are People Not Getting Married Anymore?," CNBC.com, July 19, 2023, https://www.cnbc.com/video/2023/07/19/why-are-people

-not-getting-married-anymore.html#:~:text=In%20the%20U.S.%2C%20
marriage%20has,at%20the%20University%20of%20Virginia.

9. *Merriam-Webster*, s.v. "abhor (v.)," accessed March 11, 2024, https://www
.merriam-webster.com/dictionary/abhor.

Chapter 8 The Fight for Truth

1. Thomas Sowell, "On Many Political Lessons That Need to Be Learned,"
National Review, November 1, 2016, https://www.nationalreview.com/2016/11
/thomas-sowell-thoughts-about-political-cultural-scene-2016/.

2. Katie Mettler, "Hillary Clinton Just Said It, but 'The Future Is Female'
Began as a 1970s Lesbian Separatist Slogan," *The Washington Post*, February 8,
2017, https://www.washingtonpost.com/news/morning-mix/wp/2017/02/08
/hillary-clinton-just-said-it-but-the-future-is-female-began-as-a-1970s-lesbian
-separatist-slogan/.

3. "Disparities in Suicide," Centers for Disease Control and Prevention,
accessed December 21, 2023, https://www.cdc.gov/suicide/facts/disparities
-in-suicide.html.

4. Rachel Roubein, "Suicides Are Spiking among Young Men," *Washington
Post*, September 30, 2022, https://www.washingtonpost.com/politics/2022/09
/30/suicides-are-spiking-among-young-men/.

5. Carrie Gress, *The End of Woman: How Smashing the Patriarchy Has Destroyed Us* (Washington, DC: Regnery Publishing, 2023), xxiv.

6. Gress, *End of Woman*, xxiv.

7. Selwyn Duke, "Stopping Truth at the Border," *RenewAmerica*, May 6, 2009,
http://www.renewamerica.com/columns/duke/090506.

8. Francesca Menato, "Is Lying Making Your Muscles Weaker?," July 24,
2018, *Women's Health*, https://www.womenshealthmag.com/uk/health/mental
-health/a704381/is-lying-making-your-muscles-weaker/.

9. Thomas Paine, *Common Sense*, ed. Richard Beeman (New York: Penguin
Books, 2012), 3.

Chapter 9 The Fight to Find Your Voice

1. Egard Watches, "Erased: A Message to Woke Corporate America (Nike
and Budweiser)," YouTube, April 14, 2023, ad, 1:19, https://www.youtube.com
/watch?v=H5XrTxzr2Wg.

2. Ian Janssen, Steven B. Heymsfield, ZiMian Wang, and Robert Ross et al.,
"Skeletal Muscle Mass and Distribution in 468 Men and Women Aged 18–88
Yr.," *Journal of Applied Physiology* 89, no. 1 (2000): 81–88, https://doi.org/10
.1152/jappl.2000.89.1.81.

3. Bryndís Blackadder, "Trans-Identified Male Student Wins 'Fastest Sophomore Girl' Title at Maine Race Meet," Reduxx, October 23, 2023, https://
reduxx.info/trans-identified-male-student-wins-fastest-sophomore-girl-title
-at-maine-race-meet/; Steve Craig, "Transgender Girl Makes History with
Victory at Cross Country Regional," *Portland Press Herald*, updated October

21, 2023, https://www.pressherald.com/2023/10/21/transgender-girl-makes-history-with-victory-at-cross-country-regional/.

4. Melissa Koenig, "School Stands by Trans Basketball Player Accused of Hurting Opposing Girls, Blasts 'Harmful' Criticism," *New York Post*, February 28, 2024, https://nypost.com/2024/02/28/sports/school-stands-by-trans-basketball-player-accused-of-hurting-opposing-girls-blasts-harmful-criticism/.

5. Cornelius Tacitus, *The Annals*, book 15, ch. 44, ed. Alfred John Church and William Jackson Brodribb, Perseus Digital Library, accessed November 7, 2023, https://www.perseus.tufts.edu/hopper/text?doc=Perseus%3Atext%3A1999.02.0078%3Abook%3D15%3Achapter%3D44.

6. *The Satires of Juvenal, Persius, Sulpicia, and Lucilius*, trans. Lewis Evans and William Gifford, Project Gutenberg, accessed November 7, 2023, https://www.gutenberg.org/files/50657/50657-h/50657-h.htm#Page_1.

7. Elie Wiesel, foreword to *The Courage to Care: Rescuers of Jews during the Holocaust*, ed. Carol Rittner and Sondra Myers (New York: New York University Press, 1986), x.

8. Stanisław Jerzy Lec, *More Unkempt Thoughts*, trans. Jack Galazka (New York: Funk & Wagnalls, 1968), 9.

Chapter 10 The Fight for Common Sense and Common Language

1. *Merriam-Webster*, s.v. "common sense (n.)," accessed January 22, 2024, https://www.merriam-webster.com/dictionary/common%20sense.

2. *Voltaire's Philosophical Dictionary* (New York: Carlton House, 1950; Project Gutenberg, 2006), 78, https://www.gutenberg.org/files/18569/18569-h/18569-h.htm.

3. Phyllis Schlafly, "Setback for the Transgender Agenda," Eagle Forum, August 31, 2016, https://eagleforum.org/publications/column/setback-for-the-transgender-agenda.html.

4. Megyn Kelly, "14-Year-Old Irish Girl Speaks Out on Biological Reality and Trans Indoctrination to Megyn Kelly," YouTube video, posted April 28, 2023, https://www.youtube.com/watch?v=KRvAcEm2v3c.

5. J. K. Rowling (@jk_rowling), Twitter post, June 6, 2020, 6:02 p.m., https://twitter.com/jk_rowling/status/1269389298664701952?lang=en.

6. Nelson Mandela, "Address at Worcester Station," speech, Worcester, South Africa, September 27, 1997, The Nelson Mandela Foundation Archive, https://atom.nelsonmandela.org/index.php/za-com-mr-s-511.

7. The Daily Wire (@realDailyWire), "Pro-Choice Activist Tries to Convince @michaeljknowles to Say 'Pregnant People' Instead of 'Mothers,'" X (formerly Twitter) video, December 7, 2022, https://twitter.com/realDailyWire/status/1600594242040201217?lang=en.

8. "Pronouns and Inclusive Language," LGBTQIA Resource Center, accessed March 12, 2024, https://lgbtqia.ucdavis.edu/educated/pronouns-inclusive-language.

9. Wikipedia, s.v. "doublespeak," last modified October 15, 2023, https://en .wikipedia.org/wiki/Doublespeak.

10. George Orwell, *1984* (New York: Harcourt, 1949), 5.

11. This quotation is often attributed to Saul Alinsky in *Rules for Radicals* but does not appear there. It seems to be a riff on George Orwell's "who controls the past . . . controls the future; who controls the present controls the past" (*1984*, 37).

12. *Merriam-Webster*, s.v. "language (n.)," accessed January 22, 2024, https:// www.merriam-webster.com/dictionary/language, emphasis added.

13. Jordan B. Peterson, *12 Rules for Life* (Toronto: Random House, 2018), 250.

14. George Orwell, "Politics and the English Language," The Orwell Foundation, accessed December 21, 2023, https://www.orwellfoundation.com/the -orwell-foundation/orwell/essays-and-other-works/politics-and-the-english -language/.

15. *Merriam-Webster*, s.v. "pervert (v.)," accessed January 22, 2024, https:// www.merriam-webster.com/dictionary/pervert.

16. *Merriam-Webster*, s.v. "nonsense (n.)," accessed January 22, 2024, https:// www.merriam-webster.com/dictionary/nonsense.

Chapter 11 The Cultural Fight for Female

1. Andrew Milne, "How a Teenage Boy Named Sporus Became Empress of Rome under Nero's Rule," All That's Interesting, August 25, 2020, https:// allthatsinteresting.com/sporus.

2. Brianna January, "Joe Rogan and Guest Discuss Whether Trans People Are a Sign of 'the End of America,'" Media Matters for America, September 18, 2020, https://www.mediamatters.org/joe-rogan-experience/joe-rogan-and -guest-discuss-whether-trans-people-are-sign-end-america.

3. George Santayana, *The Life of Reason: The Phases of Human Progress*, Project Gutenberg, last updated March 10, 2021, https://www.gutenberg.org /files/15000/15000-h/15000-h.htm.

4. *Merriam-Webster*, s.v. "cis- (prefix)," accessed January 22, 2024, https:// www.merriam-webster.com/dictionary/cis-.

5. *Merriam-Webster*, s.v. "trans- (prefix)," accessed January 22, 2024, https:// www.merriam-webster.com/dictionary/trans-.

6. American Psychiatric Association, *Diagnostic and Statistical Manual of Mental Disorders*, 5th ed., text revision (Washington, DC: American Psychiatric Association, 2022), 511–20.

7. American Psychiatric Association, *Diagnostic and Statistical Manual of Mental Disorders*, 5th ed. (Washington, DC: American Psychiatric Association, 2013), 454.

8. David Brown, "Seven Sex Attacks in Women's Jail by Transgender Convicts," *The Times*, May 11, 2020, https://www.thetimes.co.uk/article/seven-sex -attacks-in-womens-jails-by-transgender-convicts-cx9m8zqpg; and Salvador

Rizzo, "Victim of School Bathroom Sexual Assault Sues Va. School District," *The Washington Post*, October 5, 2023, https://www.washingtonpost.com/education/2023/10/05/loudoun-sexual-assault-stone-bridge/.

9. Morgonn McMichael, "Trans-Identified Student Attacks Female in Halls of Oregon Middle School," Turning Point USA, September 28, 2023, https://www.tpusa.com/live/trans-identified-student-attacks-female-in-halls-of-oregon-middle-school.

10. "Trans Teen Makes History as Homecoming Queen," Represented by CNN, accessed November 6, 2023, video, 1:54, https://www.cnn.com/videos/us/2021/10/05/transgender-homecoming-queen-florida-high-school-affil-pkg-vpx.wesh; and Mike Stunson, "LGBTQ+ Students Win Ohio Prom King and Queen in 'Iconic Moment.' Then Came the Vitriol," *Miami Herald*, May 3, 2023, https://www.miamiherald.com/news/nation-world/national/article275015231.html.

11. Kristina Watrobski, "Dylan Mulvaney Named 'Woman of the Year' by British Magazine," NBC Montana, October 12, 2023, https://nbcmontana.com/news/nation-world/dylan-mulvaney-named-woman-of-the-year-by-british-magazine-some-people-dont-see-me-as-a-woman-lgbt-transgender-trans-bud-light-anheuser-busch-beer-attitude-magazine; and Suzette Hackney, "'Be True to Yourself': A Message from the Nation's Highest-Ranking Openly Transgender Official," *USA Today*, March 13, 2022, https://www.usatoday.com/in-depth/opinion/2022/03/13/rachel-levine-honoree-usa-today-women-of-the-year/6600134001/.

12. Christy Choi, "Miss Universe Will Feature Two Trans Contestants for the First Time," CNN, October 13, 2023, https://www.cnn.com/style/miss-universe-trans-contestants-netherlands-portugal/index.html; Hannah Malach, "Miss Universe R'Bonney Gabriel Crowns First Transgender Winner of Miss Netherlands," Women's Wear Daily, July 10, 2023, https://wwd.com/pop-culture/celebrity-news/miss-universe-transgender-rikkie-kolle-miss-netherlands-1235738824/.

13. G. K. Chesterton, quoted in the introduction to Charles Dickens, *The Life and Adventures of Nicholas Nickleby* (London: J.M. Dent & Co, 1907), viii.

14. David K. Li, Erik Ortiz, and Marlene Lenthang, "Police Chief Tells NBC News a Sense of 'Resentment' May Have Fueled Nashville Shooter's Attack at Former School," *NBC News*, March 27, 2023, https://www.nbcnews.com/news/us-news/nashville-christian-school-shooter-appears-former-student-police-chief-rcna76876.

15. Hannah Natanson and Moriah Balingit, "Caught in the Culture Wars, Teachers Are Being Forced from Their Jobs," *The Washington Post*, June 16, 2022, https://www.washingtonpost.com/education/2022/06/16/teacher-resignations-firings-culture-wars/.

16. Joshua Q. Nelson, "11-Year-Old Reads Aloud from 'Pornographic' Book He Checked Out from Library at School Board Meeting," *New York Post*, February 28, 2023, https://nypost.com/2023/02/28/knox-zajac-reads-aloud-from-pornographic-book-at-school-board-meeting/.

17. Nikolas Lanum, "Man Forcibly Removed from School Board Meeting by Security While Reading from LGBTQ Book: 'Unconstitutional,'" Fox News, August 23, 2023, https://www.foxnews.com/media/man-forcibly-removed-school -board-meeting-security-reading-lgbtq-book-unconstitutional.

18. UCLA School of Law, "New Estimates Show 300,000 Youth Ages 13–17 Identify as Transgender in the US," The Williams Institute press release, June 10, 2022, https://williamsinstitute.law.ucla.edu/press/transgender-estimate -press-release/.

Chapter 12 The Fight against Idols

1. *Merriam-Webster*, s.v. "idol (n.)," accessed January 24, 2024, https://www .merriam-webster.com/dictionary/idol.

2. Fyodor Dostoevsky, *The Brothers Karamazov*, Bantam Classics ed. (1880; repr., New York: Bantam Dell, 2003), 419.

3. Charles Kingsley, *Alton Locke, Tailor and Poet: An Autobiography* (Oxford, 1856; Project Gutenberg, 2016), Prefatory Memoir, https://www.gutenberg.org /cache/epub/8374/pg8374-images.html.

Chapter 13 The Fight for Female Heroes

1. *Alice in Wonderland*, directed by Tim Burton (Burbank, CA: Walt Disney Studios Motion Pictures, 2010), DVD.

2. G. Michael Hopf, *Those Who Remain: A Postapocalyptic Novel* (self-pub., 2016), 18.

3. Jordan B. Peterson, "Tyrant Contra God Biblical Series: Exodus Episode 1," 23:37–26:17, Daily Wire, November 25, 2022, https://www.youtube .com/watch?v=GEASnFvLxhU; Dovie Schochet, "Who Were Shifra and Puah, the 'Hebrew Midwives'?," accessed January 24, 2024, https://www.chabad.org /parshah/article_cdo/aid/3555182/jewish/Who-Were-Shifra-and-Puah-the -Hebrew-Midwives.htm; Shira Schechter (moderator), "Were Shiphrah and Puah the First Righteous Gentiles?," The Israel Bible, December 19, 2021, https:// theisraelbible.com/were-shiphrah-and-puah-the-first-righteous-gentiles/.

Lisa Bevere

is an internationally known speaker and the *New York Times* bestselling author of *Without Rival, Fiercely Loved, Godmothers, Strong, Girls with Swords, Lioness Arising,* and more. She cohosts the podcast *Conversations with John & Lisa Bevere,* is a frequent guest on *At Home with the Beveres,* and hosts *The Fight for Female* podcast. She cofounded Messenger International, which has given away more than sixty-five million resources and launched MessengerX, a discipleship app that reaches 238 countries in 129 languages. Lisa has empowered women for more than forty years and has been featured on *Life Today, Better Together,* Hallmark's *Home and Family,* the *Dream Big Podcast with Bob Goff and Friends,* and *That Sounds Fun with Annie F. Downs,* as well as in *Relevant* magazine and more. A cancer survivor and bold truth teller, Lisa has been married to her husband, John, for over forty years, and together they have four sons and nine grandchildren.

Connect with Lisa:

 LisaBevere.com   LisaBevere

 LisaBevere   LisaBevere

 LisaBevere